Industrial America:
The Environment and Social Problems, 1865-1920

Stanley S. Graham

23.249

The Rand McNally Series on the History of American Thought and Culture

Industrial America: The Environment and Social Problems, 1865-1920

H. Wayne Morgan
University of Oklahoma, Norman

Rand McNally College Publishing Company · Chicago

The Rand McNally Series on the History of American Thought and Culture

David D. Van Tassel, series editor

Editor's Preface

The distribution of wealth in America in 1970 was exactly the same as it was in 1900. In proportion to the size of the population, the problems of the environment—air pollution, water and noise pollution, population control, crime, poverty, and even the generation gap—were all much the same as they are today. What is more, as this collection of contemporary articles and essays reveals, people were well aware of these problems, suggested and even attempted solutions, yet the problems persisted. The revelation of the long history of social problems and the general failure to solve them should raise questions about the nature and efficacy of reform during the progressive era, about American reform in general, indeed about the cultural values of the whole society.

An important key to understanding a culture is in knowing how it perceives its problems and in what ways it goes about solving them. *Industrial America* supplies that key through carefully selected contemporary essays which reveal the criteria, the scale of values of the culture of an urban-industrial society newly emerged from a chrysalis of agrarian rusticity. This volume aims to fulfill a major goal of the Rand McNally Series on the History of American Thought and Culture, which is to help the general student to understand intellectual and cultural developments during significant periods in American history. It also furnishes background for other volumes in the Series, which are original syntheses embracing chronological periods characterized by a dominant pattern of ideas or social movements. The selections in this book represent some, but by no means all, of the social problems as they were seen by those who lived during the period. When the reader examines them, we hope that he will not merely note what problems Americans faced, but how they saw them.

DAVID D. VAN TASSEL

Introduction

In 1860, the United States was a modest agrarian country; in 1920 she was the richest and most powerful nation in the world. That growth was most obvious in the statistics Americans loved to quote which charted huge increases in the production of goods and services, the extension of facilities of all kinds, and the invention of luxuries and labor-saving devices.

Firm believers in progress, long accustomed to the new and novel, Americans accepted the concrete results of industrial expansion without much question. They were less certain in assessing the origin and management of unexpected social problems and tensions. A new communications revolution spurred economic growth and scientific discovery, but its most potent impact was intangible. Better and more widespread information inevitably created public awareness of issues that had been private a generation earlier. Discussions of drug abuse, the conflicts of youth with elders, and whether to limit the inquiring mind in education became national concerns. Affluence brought comfort; it did not apparently bring satisfaction. A people who professed to love change, became apprehensive about the direction and rate of that change as it affected personal tastes and values.

The human reactions to the new world order of the late nineteenth century remain as interesting as the problems involved. The ways in which men perceive both threats and hopes determine their responses. Change is the law of life, but social and environmental problems have a special on-going quality. Every reform may produce new problems; and every technical question impinges on human feelings, often with unpredictable results. These readings hopefully will show the importance of the historical roots of some modern problems, and how earlier men reacted to their challenges.

H. WAYNE MORGAN

University of Oklahoma

Contents

Part I

The New Education

The New Education

The post-Civil War era accepted educational reform as part of a general expansion of and faith in scientific knowledge. The older college that emphasized classical learning gave way to a new university that combined technical expertise and humanism. The universities that developed in the 1880s and 1890s responded directly to an industrial society's demands for information and trained talent in all fields.

Universities thus entered into the world's work, and inevitably became involved in the world's quarrels. Politicians and overseers complained of education's insatiable costs, especially in technical fields. Educators debated how to balance science and the humanities. Was it profitable to have skilled engineers who knew no classical literature? Were students really educated if their English was weak? How much remedial work should higher education do? How could educators avoid producing only an elite? Most new universities adopted a typical American compromise: a system of student-chosen electives grouped around a core of required subjects, all designed to "round out" a man with expert skills.

College enrollments climbed, but only a small percentage of the country's young people was involved in the new education. They and society considered education a privilege, not a right. The new

3

type of student attracted a good deal of attention, mostly favorable, since he seemed to be heir to an ever-expanding future.

Most disaffection among students—and the cause of most hostility toward them—stemmed from personal conduct rather than differences over social questions. Student violence, especially in small communities, was frequent, but usually consisted of "tearing up the town," or destroying property out of frustration and boredom. Parents, administrators, and apprehensive citizens were concerned about drinking, frivolity, and various forms of sublimated sexual activity. An occasional critic lambasted a campus for being socialistic or immoral, but the concept of higher education escaped general censure.

The new universities produced a wide range of scientists and technicians for business and industry. They also enriched the agricultural sector, enlarged and modernized the nation's teaching staff, and trained experts for university research. That success obscured the failure to fuse the conflicting purposes of higher education. Intellectuals naturally sought knowledge for its own sake, implying the right to examine any proposition without extra-campus control. This sometimes ran counter to society's belief that education served the taxpayer by promoting the generally accepted social ethic and avoiding controversy. Educators desired to expand the individual student's life, but many students sought a degree chiefly to enhance their social status and income. Administrators had to mollify a diverse constituency of faculty, students, alumni, the community, and donors in the form of politicians or wealthy individuals. These and other tensions were part of a new "higher education," and of a society committed to change but attached to old ideas which that education inevitably challenged.

Chapter 1

Some Old-Fashioned Doubts About New-Fashioned Education

L. B. R. Briggs

"Doubts" is my title, not "Views"; and, as this title indicates, my paper is the expression of a mood rather than of a conviction. A mere observer of educational methods is often bothered by doubts as to the relative value of the old educational product and of the new. The new product, the educated man of today, is, in some measure, the necessity of the time. The demands of a special calling require preparation so early and so long that the all-round man—that invaluable species which has leavened and civilized all society—bids fair to be soon as extinct as the dodo. No one denies that the rare being who, in spite of the elective principle, persists in getting a general education first and a special one later, is a man of more power than if he had been driven through a general education by some other will than his own; yet with the kindergarten at one end of our education and with the elective system at

---

Excerpted from L. B. R. Briggs, "Some Old-Fashioned Doubts About New-Fashioned Education," in *Atlantic Monthly*, 86 (October, 1900), 463–470.

the other, we see, or seem to see, a falling off in the vigor with which men attack distasteful but useful things—a shrinking from the old, resolute education.

The new education has made three discoveries:

1. Education should always recognize the fitness of different minds for different work.

2. The process of education need not be, and should not be, forbidding.

3. In earlier systems of education, natural science had not a fair place.

No wonder that the new education seems to some men a proclamation of freedom. The elective system, with its branches and connections, is the natural reaction from the unintelligently rigid ignoring of mental difference in individuals. Its fundamental idea is practical, and at times inspiring. When there are so many more things worth knowing than anybody can master, to force everybody through a limited number of definite tasks before calling him educated, to make him give years to studies in which he may be a dunce, without a glimpse (except stolen glimpses) of other studies for which he may have peculiar aptitude, seems flying in the face of Providence. A classmate of mine earned (so he says) three hundred dollars in teaching a boy, who is now a distinguished physician, to spell "biscuit"; and another classmate taught a boy Greek for three months, at the end of which time the boy's knowledge of that language was summed up in the words "iota scrubscript." In the first of these cases, not much may be said for forcing spelling on the pupil; in the second, not much for forcing Greek. Again, people are more interesting for being different—for not being put through the same mill. Uneducated country people, for example, are far more interesting, far more individual, than meagerly educated city people (such as most of the salesmen in a large shop), or than semi-educated school teachers who are graduates of some one inferior normal school. We do not want men to be alike. We cannot make them alike; why do we try? If we wish to raise cranberries and beans, and own a peat swamp and a sand hill, we give up the swamp to the berries and the hill to the beans, and make no effort to raise both things in both kinds of soil. Why not let each man do what nature says he was made for? Why beat his head on a stone wall—a process that cannot be good for his mind? The old plan of learning the whole Latin grammar by heart was to some minds torture. Why should the early exercise of our powers and the training of those powers to higher service be repellent or even austere? Life is hard enough without our wantonly making it harder; let us suffer our boys and girls to *enjoy* education. Again, here is the earth we live on; here are the birds and the flowers: why shut out the study of these for Greek, Latin, and mathematics? Are the humanities human? Is mathematics either so agreeable or so useful as botany or zoölogy?

Every one of these questions is emancipatory; but the emancipation may be carried too far. Look, for example, at the elective system. No persons lay themselves open more recklessly to *reductio ad absurdum* than advocates of the elective system. Everybody believes in the elective system at some stage of education; the question is where to begin: yet extension after extension is advocated on general grounds of liberty (such liberty, by the way, as nobody has in active life); and propositions are brought forward which, if we accept them, give the elective system no logical end. Down it goes, through college, high school, and grammar school, till not even the alphabet can stop it.

Doubt I. Are we sure that we do not begin the elective system too early, or that we shall not soon begin it too early?

The attempt to make education less forbidding has called forth various devices, among them the method of teaching children to read without teaching them to spell; and the kindergarten is responsible for various attempts to make children believe they are playing games when they are, or should be, studying. . . .

A modern textbook on the study of language remarks that in walking out we see various kinds of birds—sparrows, robins, hens, and what not; and that just as there are various kinds of birds, so there are various kinds of words—nouns, verbs, adjectives. I see signs of a reaction from these debilitated methods—in particular from the method which teaches children reading without spelling; but the effect of these methods is with us still.

Doubt II. Are we sure that the enjoyment which we wish to put into education is sufficiently robust?

I may teach a boy to saw wood by suggesting that we play "Education in Cuba." We may imagine ourselves a committee for supplying the island with as many teachers as possible, both men and women. Oak sticks will furnish men, and pine sticks women (the softer sex); every sawing will make one more teacher, and every sawing through a knot a superintendent. This clever scheme has at least the merit of an undisguised attempt to make a hard job less disagreeable, and does not interfere with the clear understanding on the boy's part that he is sawing wood to help the family; just as Meg, Jo, Beth, and Amy, when they called the four hems Europe, Asia, Africa, and America, and talked about each continent as they went along, knew perfectly well that they were working. No imaginative device, however feeble, will take away the manliness of a boy who knows that work is work, and makes play of it when he honestly can; but nothing debilitates a boy more effectively than the notion that teachers exist for his amusement, and that if education does not allure him so much the worse for education.

As to natural science, I admit that it had not in the old-fashioned programmes a dignified place—such a place as would be given to it by the Committee of Ten; yet natural science may not even now have proved its equality with classics and mathematics as a disciplinary subject for boys and girls. The Committee of Ten maintained the proposition that all studies are born free and equal— possibly with an inkling that the new studies are, so to speak, freer and more equal than the old. Any one who clings to the old studies as a better foundation for training is told that his doctrine contradicts the principles of the Committee of Ten: but even this does not satisfy him; for he may not be sure of the basis for the committee's conclusions. If the earth rests on an elephant, and the elephant rests on a tortoise, the tortoise is a good tortoise, but still we need to know what the tortoise rests on.

Again, we are told—and if I am not mistaken, we are told by enthusiastic advocates of new methods—that the object of education is not knowledge so much as power; in Greek, for example, we no longer ask a boy to know three books of the Iliad, "omitting the Catalogue of the Ships;" we ask him to translate Homer at sight: yet modern doctrine fails to see, except in glimpses, that no better way of gaining power has yet been discovered than the overcoming of difficulties. The fear old-fashioned people have about new-fashioned education is that too much depends on whim, and that whim may by born of indolence. . . .

So far what I have said is chiefly theory; but the *a priori* reasoning is supported by painful signs—by crude specialists that one shudders to think of as educated men (learned men doubtless, but not educated men); by hundreds of students who lack the very underpinning of education, who are so far from knowing the first lesson of training—namely, that to be happy and successful they must get interested in what they have to do, and that doing it regularly and earnestly means getting interested—so far from knowing this, that they sit in front of a book helpless to effect any useful transfer of the author's mind to theirs. Brought up to feel that the teacher must interest them, they have become so reduced that they would like, as it were, to lie in bed, and have their studies sent up to them. Unwittingly the new-fashioned education encourages their indolence. I remember talking some years ago with a student who was fond of chemistry, but whose habits of work, as I saw them in another subject, were shiftless and slack. I tried to show him the necessity, even for his chemistry, of habitual accuracy in thought and expression; and at last I told him that, though the position he took might do for a genius, it would not do for ordinary men like himself and me. He replied that he had rather be anything than an ordinary man. What he is now, I do not know. Another student refused to take pains with his English because, as he said, he had been brought up among people who spoke English well "by intuition." This intuitive English is often picturesque and winning; but it is seldom capable of difficult work.

How many boys know what will best develop their minds? How many parents, even if themselves educated, can resist the combined pressure of boys and plausible new-fashioned educators? Even the youth who wants the old prescribed curriculum cannot get it; he may choose the old studies, but not the old instruction. Instruction under an elective system is aimed at the specialist. In elective mathematics, for example, the non-mathematical student who takes the study for self-discipline finds the instruction too high for him; indeed, he finds no encouragement for electing mathematics at all. The new system holds that the study should follow the bent of the mind rather than that the mind should bend itself to follow the study. As a result, prescribed work, so far as it exists under an elective system, is regarded by many students as

folly, and if difficult, as persecution. When the writing of forensics
—argumentative work which involved hard thinking—was prescribed in Harvard College, no work in the College was done less
honestly. Students would often defend themselves for cheating in
this study because it was "really too hard for a prescribed subject."
I know I am using a two-edged argument: does it show how the
new system weakens mental fibre, or how the old system encourages dishonesty? Different men will give different answers. As to
forensics, we may contrast with the spirit of the students the spirit
of the man who did most for the study. A trained instructor, whose
peculiar interest lay elsewhere, was asked to undertake the difficult and repellent task of teaching prescribed argumentative composition. What resulted is what always results when a trained man
makes up his mind to do a piece of work as well as he can—
genuine enthusiasm for the subject; and the instructor who expected to feel only a forced interest in argumentative composition
has become an authority in it.

I know that often the idler bestirs himself, fired by enthusiasm
in his chosen subject; and that then he sees the meaning, and even
the beauty, of drudgery: but the drudgery is less easy, because he
has never before learned to drudge with enthusiasm, or even with
the fidelity which may in time beget enthusiasm; because he never
trained his memory in childhood, when memory is trained best;
because he has always, from kindergarten to college, been treated
deferentially; because he has transferred the elective system from
studies to life. "I see in the new system," said a father the other
day, "nothing to establish the habit of application—the most valuable habit of all." "There is nothing," said the teacher with whom
he was talking, "unless the student gets interested in some study."
"Yes," said the father, "he may strike something that interests
him; but it seems dreadfully unscientific to leave it all to chance."

Doubt III, related to Doubt I. Do we not see in the men educated according to modern methods, such a weakness in attacking
difficulties as may indicate that we should be slow to let the secondary school march in the path of the college and the grammar
school follow close behind?

Another doubt about new-fashioned education I have been glad to see expressed in recent numbers of *The Nation*. It concerns what is expected of teachers; it concerns the abnormal value set on textbooks, and, I may add, the abnormal value set by some institutions on the higher degrees. We frequently hear it said of a teacher that he has taught for many years but has "produced" nothing; and this often means that he has never written a textbook. I would not undervalue textbooks as a practical result of experience in teaching: but the teacher's first business is to teach —writing is a secondary affair; and, as a rule, the best part of a teacher's production is what he produces in the minds and in the characters of his pupils. Few of the great teachers, whether of schools or of colleges, are remembered through their textbooks. Dr. Arnold of Rugby wrote textbooks (some of them bad ones); but it was not textbooks that gave Dr. Arnold his hold on English boys. The late Dr. Henry Coit had, we hear, marvelous insight into a boy's character, and marvelous power over every boy who was near him; but we never hear of his textbooks—if, indeed, he wrote any. Nor is it through textbooks that we know Dr. Bancroft of Andover, Mr. Amen of Exeter, and Mr. Peabody of Groton. The new education lays so much stress on writing and on investigation, and on theses as the result of investigation, and on originality in these theses, that it seems sometimes to encourage a young man in maintaining a proposition of which the sole value lies in its novelty (no one having been unwise enough to maintain it before), and in defending that proposition by a Germanized thesis, "Monstrum horrendum, informe, ingens, cui lumen ademptum." Such theses, I suspect, have more than once been accepted for higher degrees; yet higher degrees won through them leave the winner farther from the best qualities of a teacher, remote from men and still more remote from boys. It was a relief the other day to hear a headmaster say, "I am looking for an under teacher. I want first a *man,* and next a man to teach." It is a relief, also, to see the marked success of several schoolmasters whose preparation for teaching consists first in manliness, and secondly in only a moderate amount of learning. That a teacher should know his subject is obvious; nothing, not even new-fashioned instruction in methods of teaching, will make up for ignorance of the subject itself: but the man of intelligence and self-sacrifice who bends his energy to teaching boys will soon get enough scholarship for the purpose; whereas no amount of scholarship can make up for the want of intelligence and self-sacrifice.

Doubt IV. While fitting the study to the boy, have we been unfitting the teacher for him?

Obviously the new education throws a tremendous responsibility on teachers. We see why it should; and all of us who are familiar with the inner working of a modern school or a modern college know that it does. How is it training the new generation for this responsibility? In some ways admirably. It tries to show that teaching is not a haphazard affair, but a subject for investigation and study; it tries to show how libraries should be used, and how original investigation should be conducted: but old-fashioned people doubt whether it gives due weight to the maxim that Professor Bowen used to repeat so often, "The foundation must be stronger than the superstructure." They doubt whether teachers, themselves educated "along the lines of least resistance," can stand the strain of modern teaching. As a relief from wooden teaching and wooden learning, the new education deserves all gratitude. No one is so conservative as to prefer a dull teacher to an interesting one because the dull teacher offers more obstacles to learning. In this matter, as in all other matters of education, the question is not whether we should be altogether old-fashioned or altogether new-fashioned (we may be "alike fantastic if too new or old"): the question is where the old should stop and the new begin.

Doubt V. In emancipation from the evils of the old, may we not be rushing into another servitude almost or quite as dangerous as the first?

I have often used the word "training." Now what is training, and what is the peculiar characteristic of the trained mind? Training is the discipline that teaches a man to set labor above whim; to develop the less promising parts of his mind as well as the more promising; to make five talents ten and two five; to see that in his specialty he shall work better and enjoy more for knowing something outside of his specialty; to recognize the connection between present toil and future attainment, so that the hope of future attainment creates pleasure in present toil; to understand that nothing can be mastered without drudgery, and that drudgery in preparation for service is not only respectable but beautiful; to be interested in every study, no matter how forbidding; to work steadily and resolutely until, through long practice—and, it may be, after many failures—he is trusted to do the right thing, or something near it, mechanically, just as the trained pianist instinctively touches the right note. Training is all this and more. Why should we be content to let so many of our boys get their best discipline not from study but from athletics?

"But the new education," you say, "is in some ways more general than the old. From the start it opens to eager eyes all the beautiful world of science; little children get glimpses into subjects of which old-fashioned little children never heard." This is too true. Old-fashioned people have old-fashioned doubts about what seems to them a showy, all-round substitute for education—a sort of bluff at general culture, such as we see when children, at great expense to their schools (the new education is almost ruinously expensive), dissipate their minds by studying a little of everything. I was delighted to hear Professor Grandgent say not long ago, "The curse of modern education is multiplication of subjects and painless methods." I suspect that in another generation we may even overdo the "enriching" of the grammar school. I do not undervalue the pleasure and the profit of what is called "a bowing acquaintance" with a variety of subjects: the mistake is to accept such an acquaintance as education.

The early specialization as to which I have expressed doubt is made almost necessary by the advance of learning, the shortness of life, and the leanness of pocketbooks. The false general education is never necessary. People call it broad, but there is a big fallacy in the word "broad." A horizontal line is no broader than a perpendicular one. Just so the line of study may stretch across many subjects, and be quite as narrow as if it really penetrated one. I still doubt whether we can do better for our children than, first, to drill them in a few subjects, mostly old ones; then to give them a modest general education in college, or in all but the last year or two of college; then to let them specialize as energetically as they can (but not exclusively), and throughout to keep in their minds not pleasure only, but the stern Lawgiver who wears the Godhead's most benignant grace.

Chapter 2

The University in Politics

T. D. A. Cockerell

Seeking to define the functions of a university in a few words, I have thought that we might say: *the purpose of a university is to conserve useful truth and to add to it.* It should be in some sort the axis of our intellectual and moral growth, whence proceed the flowers and fruits of achievement. This is, of course, claiming a great deal for the institution, but it must be remembered that currents flow both ways, and the so-called product of the university is really the outcome of all human progress. Perhaps a homely illustration may serve our purpose. On pleasant evenings one may see the inhabitants of suburban districts engaged in watering their gardens. Superficially, they seem to hold in their hands useful little machines, from which, by a light pressure of the fingers, they are able to project sprays of water, strong or weak, straight or spreading, at their pleasure. Now we know that the water comes from a great reservoir, and the amateur gardeners have nothing to do with its origin or the force with which it escapes from their pipes,

---

Reprinted from T. D. A. Cockerell, "The University in Politics," in *Popular Science Monthly,* 79 (August, 1911), 160–164.

beyond, indeed, contributing their share of the water rates. Nevertheless, from the standpoint of practical gardening, a mere deluge of water, unguided in its application, would be worse than useless; consequently the pipe, the nozzle, and the gardener are essential factors for any kind of success. The university would be nothing without the great reservoir of accumulated human knowledge and experience. From this it draws its material and its energy, and yet not altogether so, for its own members, day by day, contribute intellectual capital. Literally construed, our analogy of the gardener probably breaks down in every case, because there is something creative in all human activity, though it may be, and perhaps usually is, reduced to a negligible quantity. Broadly speaking, however, the resemblance is sufficient for the purposes of argument. The university is, as it were, a nozzle through which flows, under the influence of human volition, the directed and organized output of man's mental activity. In the case of the gardener, very much—in one sense everything—depends upon his judgment, his ability to direct the water where it is needed, and in the best manner. It is even so with us. I have in the definition above not said merely that the university is to conserve truth, but *useful* truth. An intensely selective process is implied, and for this the power of judgment.

Thus another definition is equally valid: *the purpose of the university is to cultivate judgment.* The untrained individual will carelessly neglect, wantonly throw away, the most precious things because he is deficient in this quality. Without judgment it is impossible to conserve and add to *useful* truth, from sheer inability to distinguish what is useful. What is the criterion of utility? Simply the common sense one, a useful truth is one which will serve some purpose, one which has pragmatic ability. We may go deeper than that, however. What purpose can truth serve? Obviously to join with other truth in a system of ideas. There is, as it were, a sociology of thought, a cooperative commonwealth of the mind, not unlike that exhibited by human society, and strictly parallel with it in development. Now in society, where all may share in the fruits of the intellect of the few, numbers and variety are necessary; so is it also with the mind, and thus judgment is not an esoteric ability conferred at random on pensive souls, but is dependent for its very livelihood on sufficient and diverse knowledge.

According to the description we have given of university functions, it must be apparent that the relation between foci of learning and public affairs is fundamental. Knowledge and judgment are the very qualities which necessarily determine the success of a politician in any broad and lasting sense. A successful public man is one who efficiently serves public ends; no other definition is possible, although, according to it, some current motions of success may be reversed. Many there are who unquestionably are successful, and likewise are public men; so there are great fools who are also men, but we do not call them great men. I think we may say without contradiction that the things the university stands for are precisely those most valuable in genuine politics, as distinguished from the mere struggle between predatory interests.

Here it will occur to many that academic bodies are somewhat arrogant, in the face of the fact that so much good knowledge and admirable judgment has resided and does reside in persons who have never been subjected to college influences. Such criticism is justly directed against claims occasionally made, but broadly speaking it has no foundation. The university is an intellectual focus, just as the church is a religious one, and from each the light spreads in all directions. It is not possible to say just where either begins or ceases. Legally, it is true, the university is a definite corporation, with particular precisely indicated members. Spiritually, intellectually, it is nothing more than the nucleus of an intellectual nebula; which nebula, in fact, is world wide, with as many nuclei as there are centers of learning, whether represented by buildings and charters or not. Thus to be a citizen of the university is ipso facto to be a citizen of the world, and the custom prevalent in some European countries of addressing all co-workers in one's subject as "dear colleague" is abundantly justified. So the university need not be ashamed to make large claims, always provided that it is really a place of intellectual and moral activity, and not a mental vacuum concealed by handsome buildings.

Many, substantially agreeing with what has been said, will declare that the university should *not* be in politics, because it cultivates knowledge and judgment, for others to *apply*. It is also often said that university professors are not practical men of affairs, being absorbed in their studies, while the world goes by unheeded. Taking the last statement first, we must confess that there is something in it. It is possible for a specialist to be doing splendid work, of the greatest advantage to mankind, without having any clear idea of the ultimate application of his discoveries, much less those in other fields. On the other hand eminent specialists are sometimes distinguished, like Huxley and Virchow, for their broad grasp of social questions and great services as publicists. Aside from these considerations, however, is the fact that the university is in a sense an intellectual baby farm, and the infant ideas nourished there are many of them not yet ready to go out in the world and do their day's work. It is about as just to complain of the inutility of new truths as it would be to blame mothers of young children in time of war, because of failure to contribute members to the army.

There is, however, one quality of great public value in which scientific men are admittedly as preeminent as the majority of present-day politicians are deficient. This is the power, or the habit, of forming so-called impartial judgments, that is, judgments based on the available evidence, not dictated by partisan or personal desires. We are only just beginning to realize that men of this class will be widely useful in the guidance of the ship of state, bringing about the transformation of much that is undesirable in the life of this nation. It is not expected that every scientific man will offer opinions on every subject; precisely because he has the quality referred to he will refuse to do this; but when he feels competent to express an opinion, after due research, it will be worth more in the consideration of the tariff, the treatment of the Filipinos, or the question of railroad regulation, than that of any political boss who ever lived. This opinion will not be impartial, in the sense of being colorless; rarely will the expert desire or contrive to sit gracefully on the fence, but it will bring to a focus the best results of human thought as applied to the matter in hand. Against all this will be cited the well-known saying that "doctors disagree." You can find an "expert," people say, to declare anything. It is true that on many important scientific questions eminent workers differ greatly, but when this is the case, those questions are considered still open for discussion. It is one of the merits of science, as against partisan politics, that she does not feel obliged to decide everything as though by infallible judgment. Many things are still in the experimental stage. It should be stated, however, that most of the alleged experts who muddle the public mind are partly or wholly pseudoscientific. A very small amount of inquiry among the citizens of the real republic of science would demonstrate this to any one.

Thus, I think the members of any university faculty should be "in politics" to the extent of being ready and anxious to help wherever they can, to come forward and fight for what they believe to be true and wise. They should also, it is almost superfluous to say, stand always for the moral and decent thing. On the other hand, speaking for myself, I do not see how any man with scientific training can be a strictly "regular" member of any political party. In some particular controversy, he may be wholly on one side, but in the long run, orthodox party service deprives him of that freedom of judgment and action which he deems so essential. Fortunately, everything indicates the breaking up of the old rigid lines; not, I believe, so much to form new ones along fresh directions of cleavage, as to allow greater freedom for the products of honest thought. Thus the initiative and referendum, by compelling people to form judgments on particular questions, will prove well worth the expense and sometimes inconvenience they may occasion.

What about the student body in politics? Its members are young and relatively inexperienced, but they are, we hope, to be the politicians of the future. They ought, at any rate, to be in training for public service. Probably the greatest criticism that future generations will make on our present educational system is this, that thought and deed are too far apart; so far, often, that the deed never follows. Everyone deplores the lack of earnest purpose shown by so many university students, and many attribute it to an absolute deficiency in the individuals concerned. Much of it, I fancy, is due to nothing more than lack of opportunity to do things; an opinion confirmed in part by the extraordinary activity shown from time to time in foolish undertakings, and in part by the excellent record in life of many men who were never considered very able in college. It is in many ways a difficult situation, yet I confess I should be willing to see our students more active in public affairs, more like those men of the universities who have always taken prominent parts in political crises in Germany. To some extent the faults of immaturity are offset by the fresh and generous attitude of one who goes to battle unwounded and unafraid. I remember how a certain writer once rejoiced that he had, when a young man, written a book. It was bold to the point of error, he would not, could not, write so now—but, after all, it had a precious quality he could never again approach.

The internal activities of the university afford scope for a good deal of political talent, but unfortunately their purposes are often petty, and their conduct sometimes reflects all too well the method prevalent in "real" politics outside. Here again, no doubt conditions are improving, and the time may come when even the most significant matters afford scope for the development of habits and points of view of the utmost moment. We have also the civic clubs, really entering into the national arena to some extent, and already doing valuable public service.

In all of this, we shall reap approximately what we sow. If, in some countries learning and possibly virtue are more highly esteemed than in our own, it is the work of those who have stood for learning and virtue, year after year, month by month, day by day. These things will not come without conscious and long-continued effort. I feel that in our anxiety for material support, we sometimes forget the essential things. It is good to have money, it is delightful to see a large and growing student body, but whatever comes of it, let us always refuse to sell our birthright for even the largest, most attractive mess of pottage.

Chapter 3

Socialism in the Colleges

Simon-pure Socialism is so ugly, so red in tooth and claw, that to be hated it needs but to be seen and understood. Yet there are so many dilutions of Socialism on the market, emotional adulterations and attenuations of the genuine brand, that the inexperienced seeker is pretty sure to have a mixture far below full strength palmed off on him, and after tasting he will be likely to say that the stuff is not so bad, after all. Socialism is offered in the guise of bland and salutary reforms; it takes the form of ethical standards, of social justice, of uplift, and of progress and happiness for all; now it is the shield that guards the poor and the helpless against the shafts of undeserved ill fortune, and now it stays the hand of the heartless oppressor. In its assumptions it is the Ten Commandments, it is the Sermon on the Mount, it is Christianity. Can we wonder that in these disguises it disarms suspicion and wins a tolerance that is already a halfway approval?

It is time that the men and women of this country awoke to an understanding of the true nature of Socialism, of what it is, what it aims to do, and how it seeks to achieve its ends. Socialism is

Reprinted from "Socialism in the Colleges," in *Century Magazine,* 86 (July, 1913), 468–470.

revolution, it is blood, it is overthrow, spoliation, and a surrender of the priceless conquests of civilization, an extinction of the noble impulses that have raised mankind out of the condition of savagery.

It is time these things were known and understood, we say; it is time that foolish misconception gave way to clear knowledge, because Socialism is everywhere sowing its seeds, because it is spreading in the land, not insidiously, but by an open propaganda; because the principles of Socialism are taking hold upon the minds of youth through teaching permitted, or in the name of "academic freedom" actually encouraged, in our schools, colleges, universities, and even in theological seminaries. And it is only here and there that from some chair of instruction a voice is heard proclaiming the truth about Socialism, examining its foundations, subjecting its system and its principles to the test of reason and common sense, and picturing forth in the clear light of experience the consequences of substituting them for the existing social order. Having permitted this poison to be instilled into the minds of their students, it is the belief of men who have observed with growing apprehension the spread of Socialistic belief, that the country's institutions of learning will be false to their duty if they fail to supply the antidote by establishing courses of instruction in which the fallacies, the falsehoods, and the dangers of Socialism shall be combatted by competent analysis in the light of history and economic truth.

No board of trustees, no faculty, can plead an excusable ignorance as to what Socialists intend. They differ as to plan and method, but they are agreed upon this foundation article of their faith:

> The Socialist program requires the public or collective ownership and operation of the principal instruments and agencies for the production and distribution of wealth—the land, mines, railroads, steamboats, telegraph and telephone lines, mills, factories, and modern machinery.

"This is the main program," says Morris Hillquit, and it "admits of no limitation, extension, or variation." The Socialist program means, then, the abolition of private property in land and in investments, the abolition of rent, profits, of the wage system, and

of competition. Some Socialists advocate confiscation by taxing at
full value—for, of course, Socialism aims at full control of the
powers of government; some, like the Industrial Workers of the
World, would have the wage earners take forcible possession of
the factories and operate them for their own account; others
would make a pretense of payment, while still others preach direct seizure. All agree that the land and the instruments of production and exchange must be taken out of the hands of private
owners and transferred to the State, and assent to that foundation
doctrine makes every Socialist a revolutionist. Obviously, it is a
revolution that could succeed only through violence and bloodshed, but the real Socialists do not shrink from the extreme. "The
safety and the hope of the country," said Victor Berger, the Socialist member of the last Congress, "will finally lie in one direction
only—that of violent and bloody revolution." He advises Socialists
to read and think, and also "have a good rifle." But the literature
of Socialism supplies proof upon proof that the capture of the
Government and of property is to be effected by violence. Hence
the Socialist's hatred of the Army, of the Navy, and of the National
Guard; hence his detestation of all manifestations of the sentiment
of patriotism.

Indeed, one of the noblest expressions of that sentiment which
our literature affords may serve as a complete demonstration of
the conflict between the doctrines of Socialism and some of the
convictions that have struck their roots deepest in our common
life. The familiar lines of Fitz-Greene Halleck's "Marco Bozzaris"
admirably serve the purpose:

> Strike, for your altars and your fires;
> Strike, for the green graves of your sires,
> God, and your native land!

Our "altars" are the symbol of our religion. "No God, no master,"
is the cry of the Socialists, and it was only after a prolonged debate
that a repudiation of religion was kept out of the Socialist platform
of 1908. Our "fires" are our homes and hearthstones. Socialism
would destroy the home. The revolting doctrine of promiscuity
was applauded, and applauded by young women of the faith, at a
recent meeting of Socialists. "The green graves of your sires"—
those words should remind us that the earliest form of title to land

was the right to enclose the graves of parents and kindred. Socialism permits no private ownership of land. "God, and your native
land"—Socialism denies the Creator and puts the red flag above
the Stars and Stripes. Could the grim meaning of this hideous
creed be brought more directly home to the minds and hearts of
American youth than by the evidence that it is a cold-blooded
negation of the fine and lofty patriotism of Halleck's adjuration?
Yet American youth by thousands are today under Socialistic
teaching and conviction. In December 1912, the Fourth Annual
Convention of the Intercollegiate Socialist Society was held in
New York. It was reported that there were fifty-nine "chapters"
of the society in as many colleges and universities, including all the
leading institutions of the country, and eleven graduate chapters.
There were between 900 and 1,000 members of the undergradu-
ate chapters, and 700 graduate members. The list of "enthusiastic
disciples of Karl Marx" among college faculties includes the names
of many professors of national repute. Socialism is at work, too, in
the schools, and it has schools of its own, and in this city its "Sunday
schools." The doctrines are put before children and youth not as
doctrines of destruction and confiscation, and of revolution by
violence and bloodshed, but as principles of ethics, of social justice,
and the common good, all leading up to the beautiful dream of the
brotherhood of man. College students are asked to consider the
working of some privately managed undertaking, and then by
plausible illustrations it is pointed out to them that the State could
perform the service much better, and thus the ground principle
of Socialism gets a lodgment in minds insufficiently informed to
detect the falsity of the teaching. In the children's schools is used
"The Socialist Primer." in which by text and pictures hatred of the
rich and well-to-do is implanted, and the working-man is presented as the helpless victim of greed and cruel oppression. The
facts of Socialism, the truth about Socialism, are open to ascertain-
ment by every college and university trustee, by every president,
by every giver of funds whose benefactions are employed in part
to support the teaching of this devil's creed that is to supplant our
old-time reverence for the altar, the hearth-fire, the family, the
graves of kindred, and the flag. There is no vital difference between Socialists. The revolutionaries of the Haywood and Debs
type and the evolutionary Socialists of the college faculties have

virtually a common faith, and tend inevitably to the acceptance of one method for its attainment.

Is this teaching of revolution and confiscation to go on? A sound course of instruction devoted to the exposure of the fallacies, the falsehoods, and the destructive purposes of Socialism in every college where it has gained a foothold, would make the student immune to its poisonous delusions. Truth is the natural shield against error, yet only here and there has its protection been extended over the endangered youth of our colleges. The teaching of false history and false science would not be tolerated anywhere. Is it less important that young men should be safeguarded against false teaching in matters that go to the very groundwork of their morality and their citizenship? The trustees, presidents, and faculties of the country's seats of learning have a duty to perform that they cannot longer neglect without inviting the sternest censure of public opinion.

Part II

Strange New Youth

Strange New Youth

Youth and age have always been conscious of each other's roles, but the awareness of youth as a separate stage of life seemed to sharpen with the arrival of the new century. The country had a youthful tone in much of its work. "Progressive" politicians were younger than the men they challenged. Industry and business welcomed young talent, and all the arts had a youthful emphasis. The new cities and campuses concentrated young people conspicuously, and Sunday supplements and special articles attested to increased interest in them.

Industrialism and prosperity also supported an array of goods, entertainments, and leisure activities for young consumers. The craze for bicycles attested to youth's restlessness and to a new means of escaping parental control. There were special fashions for young people. An emphasis on youth, which was natural in a country that prized everything new, affected advertising.

While grateful for the new, enlarged sense of life available to the maturing generation, many elders were apprehensive at youth's alleged distaste for hard work and discipline. More than ever, young people seemed knowledgeable about the world through improved education and new forms of communications. They were noticeably impatient with accepted ways. But while some young people entered into controversial social concerns such as social work, the great majority chaffed at personal restraints. The most unsettling aspect of the problem to adults was the rather sudden realization that young people seemed intent on drawing their tastes and ideals from each other and the present, rather than from their elders and the sanctified past.

Chapter 4

A Letter
to the Rising Generation

Cornelia A. P. Comer

From the dawn of time, one generation has cried reproof and
warning to the next, unheeded. "I wonder that you would still be
talking. Nobody marks you," say the young. "Did you never hear
of Cassandra?" the middle-aged retort.

Many of you young people of today have *not* heard of Cassandra, for a little Latin is no longer considered essential to your
education. This, assuredly, is not your fault. You are innocent
victims of a good many haphazard educational experiments. New
ideas in pedagogy have run amuck for the last twenty-five years.
They were introduced with much flourish of drums; they looked
well on paper; they were forthwith put into practice on the helpless young. It has taken nearly a generation to illustrate their
results in flesh and blood. Have they justified themselves in you?

The rising generation cannot spell, because it learned to read by
the word-method; it is hampered in the use of dictionaries, be-

---

Excerpted from Cornelia A. P. Comer, "A Letter to the Rising Generation," in
Atlantic Monthly, 107 (February, 1911), 145–154.

cause it never learned the alphabet; its English is slipshod and commonplace, because it does not know the sources and resources of its own language. Power over words cannot be had without some knowledge of the classics or much knowledge of the English Bible—but both are now quite out of fashion.

As an instance of the working out of some of the newer educational methods, I recall serving upon a committee to award prizes for the best essays in a certain competition where the competitors were seniors in an accredited college. In despair at the material submitted, the committee was finally forced to select as "best" the essay having the fewest grammatical errors and the smallest number of misspelled words. The one theme which showed traces of thought was positively illiterate in expression.

These deficiencies in you irritate your seniors, but the blame is theirs. Some day you will be upbraiding your instructors for withholding the simple essentials of education, and you will be training your own children differently. It is not by preference that your vocabulary lacks breadth and your speech distinction. In any case, these are minor indictments, and, when all is said, we older ones may well ask ourselves whether we find our minds such obedient, soft-footed servants of the will as to make it clear that the educational procedure of our own early days is to be indorsed without reserve.

Your seniors also find themselves irritated and depressed because modern girls are louder-voiced and more bouncing than their predecessors, and because their boy-associates are somewhat rougher and more familiar toward them than used to be thought well-bred. But even these things, distasteful as they are, should not be the ground of very bitter complaint. It requires more serious charges than these to impeach the capacity and intentions of those who are soon to be in full charge of this world. Every generation has—with one important abatement—the right to fashion its own code of manners.

The final right of each generation to its own code depends upon the inner significance of those manners. When they express such alterations in the fibre of the human creature as are detrimental to the welfare of the race, then, and perhaps then only, are our criticisms completely justified. . . .

Is the quality of the human product really falling off? That is the humiliating question you must ask yourselves. If the suspicion which runs about the world is true, then, youngsters, as you would elegantly phrase it, it is "up to you."

One of the advantages of living long in the world is that one steadily acquires an increasingly interesting point of view. Even in middle life one begins to see for one's self the evolution of things. One gets a glimpse of the procession of events, the march of the generations. The longer an intelligent being lives, the more deeply experience convinces him that there is a pattern in the tapestry of our lives, individual as well as national and racial, at whose scope we can only guess.

Yet the things we actually see and can testify to are profoundly suggestive. I know of my own knowledge how greatly the face of life in this country has altered since my own childhood. It is neither so simple nor so fine a thing as then. And the type of men of whom every small community then had at least half a dozen, the big-brained, big-hearted, "old Roman" men, whose integrity was as unquestioned as their ability, is almost extinct. Their places are cut up and filled by smaller, less able, often much less honest men. It is not that the big men have gone to the cities—for they are not there; it is not that they left no descendants—for in more cases than I care to count, the smaller, less able, less honest men are their own sons. These latter frequently make as much money in a year as their fathers did in ten, and show less character in a lifetime than their fathers did in a year.

The causes of this are too complicated to go into here, but so far as you young people just coming on the stage are concerned, the result of this change of type in American life and American men is to make life a far harder problem. The world is itself smaller; it is harder for the individual to live by his own light. The members of the body politic are much more closely knit together in the mesh of common interest today than ever before. While political scandals, graft, and greed have always existed, there never has been a time when low standards in business and politics have so assailed the honor and integrity of the people as a whole, by tempting them, through fear of loss, to acquiesce in the dishonesty of others. If better standards are to prevail, it is you who must fight their final battles. Your wisdom, patience, and moral earnestness are going to be taxed to the breaking point before those battles are won. Have you the muscle for that fight?

Evidence in regard to the falling off in the human product is necessarily fragmentary and chaotic. Let us run over a few of the points your elders have observed and recorded against you. Veteran teachers are saying that never in their experience were young people so thirstily avid of pleasure as now. "But," one urges, "it is the season when they should enjoy themselves. Young people always have—they always will." "Yes," they answer "that is true, but this is different from anything we have ever seen in the young before. They are so keen about it—so selfish, and so hard!"

Of your chosen pleasures, some are obviously corroding to the taste; to be frank, they are vulgarizing. It is a matter of ordinary comment that the children of cultivated fathers and mothers do not, nowadays, grow up the equals of their parents in refinement and cultivation. There must, then, be strong vulgarizing elements outside the home, as well as some weakness within, so to counteract and make of little worth the gentler influences of their intimate life. How can anything avail to refine children whose taste in humor is formed by the colored supplements of the Sunday paper, as their taste in entertainment is shaped by continuous vaudeville and the moving picture shows? These things are actually very large factors in children's lives today. How should they fail of their due influence on plastic human material? Where the parents at the formative age saw occasional performances of Booth, Barrett, Modjeska, and "Rip Van Winkle," the children go to vaudeville, and go almost constantly. While most vaudeville performances have one or two numbers that justify the proprietors' claim of harmless, wholesome amusement, the bulk of the programme is almost inevitably drivel, common, stupid, or inane. It may not be actually coarse, but inanity, stupidity, and commonness are even more potent as vulgarizing influences than actual coarseness. Coarseness might repel; inanity disintegrates.

"I don't approve," your fathers and mothers say anxiously, "but I hate to keep Tom and Mary at home when all the other children are allowed to go." These parents are conscientious and energetic in looking after Tom's teeth and eyes, Mary's hair, tonsils, and nasal passages, but seem utterly unconscious that mental rickets and curvature of the soul are far more deforming than crooked teeth and adenoids. . . .

When the rising generation goes into the militia, it is, old officers tell us, "soft" and incompetent, unpleasantly affected by ants and

spiders, querulous as to tents and blankets, and generally as incapable of adapting itself to the details of military life as one would
expect a flat-reared generation to be. The advocates of athletics
and manual training in our schools and colleges are doing their
utmost to counteract the tendency to make flabby, fastidious bodies which comes from too-comfortable living; but the task is huge.

Much more ado is made over this business of training the mind
and body today than ever before. From the multiplied and improved machinery of education, it would seem that we must be far
in advance of our fathers. But where are the results in improved
humanity? The plain truth seems to be that the utmost which can
be done for the child today is not enough to counterbalance the
rapidly growing disadvantages of urban life and modern conditions. Vast increase in effort and in cost does not even enable the
race to keep up with itself. Forging ahead at full speed, we are yet
dropping woefully behind.

Training is not a matter of the mind and body only. More fundamental to personality than either is the education of the soul. In
your upbringing this has been profoundly neglected—and here is
your cruelest loss. Of the generation of your fathers and mothers
it may be generally affirmed that they received their early religious training under the old régime. Their characters were shaped
by the faith of their fathers, and those characters usually remained
firm and fixed, though their minds sometimes became the sport of
opposing doctrines. They grew up in a world that was too hastily
becoming agnostic as a result of the dazzling new discoveries of
science. It was a shallow interpretation that claimed science and
religion as enemies to the death. So much is clear now. But, shallow or not, such was the thought of the seventies. The rising
generation of that day had to face it. A great many young people
then became unwilling martyrs to what they believed the logic of
the new knowledge. It was through inability to enlarge their ideas
of Him, to meet the newly disclosed facts about His universe, that
they gave up their God. They lost their faith because imagination
failed them.

The clamor and the shouting of that old war have already died
away; the breach between science and religion is healed; the
world shows more and more mysterious as our knowledge of it
widens, and we acknowledge it to be more inexplicable without

a Will behind its phenomena than with one. But that period of storm and stress had a practical result; it is incarnated in the rising generation.

In the wrack of beliefs, your parents managed to retain their ingrained principles of conduct. Not knowing what to teach you, they taught you nothing wholeheartedly. Thus you have the distinction of growing up with a spiritual training less in quantity and more diluted in quality than any "Christian" generation for nineteen hundred years. If you are agnostic-and-water, if you find nothing in the universe more stable than your own wills—what wonder? Conceived in uncertainty, brought forth in misgiving— how can such a generation be nobly militant?

Before it occurred to me to analyze your deficiencies and your predicament thus, I used to look at a good many members of the rising generation and wonder helplessly what ailed them. They were amiable, attractive, lovable even, but singularly lacking in force, personality, and the power to endure. Conceptions of conduct that were the very foundations of existence to decent people even fifteen years their seniors were to them simply unintelligible. The word "unselfishness," for instance, had vanished from their vocabularies. Of altruism, they had heard. They thought it meant giving away money if you had plenty to spare. They approved of altruism, but "self-sacrifice" was literally as Sanskrit to their ears. They demanded ease; they shirked responsibility. They did not seem able to respond to the notion of duty as human nature has always managed to respond to it before.

All this was not a matter of youth. One may be undeveloped and yet show the more clearly the stuff of which one is made. It was a matter of substance, of mass. You cannot carve a statue in the round from a thin marble slab; the useful two-by-four is valueless as framing timber for ships; you cannot make *folks* out of light weight human material.

When these young persons adopted a philosophy, it was naïve and inadequate. They talked of themselves as "socialists," but their ideas of socialism were vague. To them it was just an "ism" that was going to put the world to rights without bothering them very much to help it along. They seemed to feel that salvation would come to them by reading Whitman and G. B. S., or even the mild and uncertain Mr. H. G. Wells, and that a vague, general goodwill toward man was an ample substitute for active effort and self-sacrifice for individuals. Somebody, some day, was going to push a button, and presto! life would be soft and comfortable for everybody.

Of socialism in general I confess myself incompetent to speak. It may, or it may not, be the solution of our acutely pressing social problems. But if men are too cheap, greedy, and sordid to carry on a republic honestly, preserving that equality of opportunity which this country was founded to secure, it must be men who need reforming. The more ideal the scheme of government, the less chance it has against the inherent crookedness of human nature. In the last analysis, we are not ruled by a "government," but by our own natures objectified, moulded into institutions. Rotten men make rotten government. If we are not improving the quality of the human product, our social system is bound to grow more cruel and unjust, whatever its name or form.

"But, of course, you believe," said one pink-cheeked young socialist, expounding his doctrine, "that the world will be a great deal better when everybody has a porcelain bathtub and goes through high school. Why—why, of course, you *must* believe that!"

Dear lad, I believe nothing of the kind! You yourself have had a porcelain bathtub from your tenderest years. You also went through high school. Yet you are markedly inferior to your old grandfather in every way—shallower, feebler, more flippant, less efficient physically and even mentally, though your work is with books, and his was with flocks and herds. Frankly, I find in you nothing essential to a man. God knows what life can make of such as you. I do not. Your brand of socialism is made up of a warm heart, a weak head, and an unwillingness to assume responsibility for yourself or anybody else—in short, a desire to shirk. These elements are unpleasantly common in young socialists of my acquaintance. I know, of course, that a very passion of pity, a Christlike tenderness, brings many to that fold, but there are more of another kind. It was one of the latter who was horrified by my suggestion that he might have to care for his parents in their old age. It would interfere too much, he said, with his conception of working out his own career!

What can one say to this? The words "character" and "duty" convey absolutely nothing to young people of this type. They have not even a fair working conception of what such words mean. Did

I not dispute a whole afternoon with another young man about the necessity for character, only to learn at the end of it that he didn't know what character was. He supposed it was "something narrow and priggish—like what deacons used to be." And he, mind you, was in his twenties, and claimed, *ore rotundo,* to be a Whitmanite, a Shavian, and a socialist. Also, he was really intelligent about almost everything in life—which is the only thing it is at all needful to be intelligent about. . . .

It may easily happen that the next twenty years will prove the most interesting in the history of civilization. Armageddon is always at hand in some fashion. Nice lads with the blood of the founders of our nation in your veins, pecking away at the current literature of socialism, taking out of it imperfectly understood apologies for your temperaments and calling it philosophy—where will you be if a Great Day should really dawn? What is there in your way of thought to help you play the man in any crisis? If the footmen have wearied you, how shall you run with the horsemen? In one way or another, every generation has to fight for its life. When your turn comes, you will be tossed on the scrap-heap, shoved aside by boys of a sterner fibre and a less easy life, boys who have read less and worked more, boys who have thought to some purpose and have been willing—as you are not—to be disciplined by life. . . .

Consider the matter of your own existence and support that you accept with such nonchalant ease. Every child born into the world is paid for with literal blood, sweat, tears. That is the fixed price, and there are no bargain sales. Years of toil, months of care, hours of agony, go to your birth and rearing. What excuse have you, anyhow, for turning out flimsy, shallow, amusement-seeking creatures, when you think of the elements in your making? The price is paid gladly. That is your fathers' and mothers' part. Yours is, to be worth it. You have your own salvation to work out. It must be salvation, and it must be achieved by work. That is the law, and there is no other. . . .

No generalizations apply to all of a class. Numerically, of course, many of the rising generation are fine and competent young people, stanch, generous, right-minded, seeking to give and to get the best in life and to leave the world better than they found it. I take it, any young person who reads the *Atlantic* will have chosen this better part—but, suppose you hadn't! Suppose you discovered yourself to be one of those unfortunates herein described? Deprived of the disciplinary alphabet, multiplication table, Latin grammar; dispossessed of the English Bible, most stimulating of literary as well as of ethical inheritances; despoiled of your birthright in the religion that made your ancestors; destitute of incentives to hardihood and physical exertion; solicited to indolence by cheap amusements, to self-conceit by cheap philosophies, to greed by cheap wealth—what, then, is left for you?

Even if your predicament were, without relief, dire as this, you would at least have the chance to put up a wonderful fight. It would be so good a thing to win against those odds that one's blood tingles at the thought. But there are several elements which alter the position. For one, the lack of a definite religious training is not irreparable.

This is not a sermon, and it is for others to tell those how to find God who have not yet attained unto Him, but it is certain that the mature world around you with which you are just coming into definite relation is morally very much alive just now. That its moral awakening is not exactly on the lines of previous ones, does not make it less authentic or contagious. Unless you are prematurely case-hardened, it is bound to affect you.

Then—you are young. It is quite within your power to surprise yourselves and discomfit the middle-aged prophets of evil who write you pages of warnings. The chance of youth is always the very greatest chance in the world, the chance of the uncharted sea, of the undiscovered land.

The idealism of the young and their plasticity in the hands of their ideals have carried this old world through evil days before now. It has always been held true that so long as you are under twenty-five, you are not irrevocably committed to your own deficiencies. I wonder if you realize that for you, first among the sons of men, that period of grace has been indefinitely extended?

The brain specialists and the psychologists between them have given in the last ten years what seems conclusive proof of the servitude of the body to the Self; they have shown how, by use of the appropriate mechanism in our makeup, we can control to a degree even the automatisms of our bodies; they have demonstrated the absolute mastery of will over conduct. Those ancient foes, Heredity and Habit, can do very little against you, today, that you are not in a position to overcome. Since the world began, no human creatures have had the scientific assertion of this that you possess. Many wise and many righteous have longed to be assured of these matters, and have agonized through life without that certainty. Saints and sages have achieved by long prayer and fasting the graces that you, apparently, may attain by the easy process of a self-suggestion.

Coming as this psychological discovery does, in the middle of an age of unparalleled mechanical invention and discovery, it is almost—is it not?—as if the Creator of men had said, "It is time that these children of mine came to maturity. I will give them at last their full mastery over the earth and over the air and over the spirits of themselves. Let us see how they bear themselves under these gifts."

Thus, your responsibility for yourselves is such an utter responsibility as the race has never known. It is the ultimate challenge to human worth and human power. You dare not fail under it. I think the long generations of your fathers hold their breath to see if you do less with certainty than they have done with faith.

Chapter 5

On the Alleged Deterioration of Youth

Agatha Reynolds

Yes, Jane, I have read both the magazine articles to which you refer, and which you so feelingly indorse. In the last ten years I have also read scores of similar articles, setting forth the shortcomings of youth, and I am now quite sure that Adam and Eve were the only elderly couple this world has ever held who, for obvious reasons, did not consider that young people had changed for the worse since the days when *they* were boy and girl.

Don't think, please, that I am cherishing illusions. I am not. I am cherishing recollection instead. Of course girls are silly and selfish. "Knowledge comes, but wisdom lingers"—only the coming of knowledge is problematic, and the lingering of wisdom is a sure thing. Of course boys are wasting their opportunities. Was there ever a boy except William Pitt, Junior, who didn't waste his opportunities? But I remember what I was at seventeen; and, what is more, I remember what you were at the same age—a very pretty

Reprinted from Agatha Reynolds, "On the Alleged Deterioration of Youth," in *Century Magazine,* 82 (August, 1911), 627–628.

girl, Jane dear, but certainly no pattern to your sex; and, what is still more, I remember what Tom was before he married you. Just ask him tonight if I don't. Yet here am I, a lady not destitute of merit; and here is Tom—well, really, we are all rather proud of Tom; and here are you, the mother of four big boys so wedded to athletics that they do not even smoke. Is it for you to lament that the rising generation do not reach the high standards of our youth?

Jane, do you perchance remember the foolish and vapid flirtations which engrossed our minds and hearts? We did not play any outdoor game but croquet, and what girl could work off her superfluous and perilous energy, dawdling about a croquet ground? Do you remember the systematic deception which made possible Tom's courtship, and how you excused yourself for hoodwinking your parents by saying that they, in their time, had run away to be married? Do you remember how many of Tom's college friends drank, how many of our friends were what we somewhat proudly called "fast," and what a vulgar and demoralizing thing this fastness was? And don't you think that the trouble lay in the aloofness of older people who might have helped us had we been more friendly and less deferential, and in our not having our fair share of keen and healthy interests to keep us out of mischief?

"Never," you write, quoting from one of your disconsolate critics, "were the young so thirstily avid for pleasure as now." My dear Jane, we were just as avid in our day, only less frank, and a trifle less strenuous. Tom did not play football, but more than once he played the fool, a part suited to his joyous immaturity. We did not strive so hard to amuse ourselves—perhaps because we did not know how—but neither did we strive to improve the race, like the dear children who are now teaching sociology to factory hands, and the principles of art to slum babies, and the rights and wrongs of suffrage to the world. Please don't quote vulgar proverbs about grandmothers and eggs, because I won't listen to them. Imparting one's ignorance to one's fellow creatures may not be the highest form of usefulness; but at least the girls so engaged are avid for other things than pleasure, they are stirred by nobler impulses than the mere love of fun. For my part, I like to be instructed by my juniors. It lightens the responsibilities of age.

As to manners, well, if young people no longer affect the reverence they never felt for our advancing years, if they meet us with more candor and a trifle more of condescension, we are gainers by the change. We are admitted to a companionship which elderly ladies (and please remember that we *are* elderly in their eyes) never enjoyed before, and by which it behooves us to profit. You know Mrs. James Landon, or at least you used to know her before she left Boston. She is the most wonderful old woman in the world, eighty-seven if she is a day, and as alert, as keen, as gay, and as capable of sustaining an argument as if she were half that age. Well, the other day she complained half-humorously to me that her grandchildren (three of them were in the room) did not treat her with proper respect; whereupon Eloise Brinton's youngest daughter, who is still going to school, said: "And a precious good thing it is for you, Granny dear, that we don't. It is our disrespect which has made you the delightful old lady that you are. If we never contradicted you, and never argued with you, and never jolted you out of your ruts, you'd be a chimney-corner grandmother, as dull as dull can be. We keep you young. We treat you as if you were one of ourselves. We do you the justice of meeting you mind to mind."

There is the arrogance of youth for you, but there is also the boon which only youth can give. I hope that if ever I live to be eighty-seven, somebody else's grandchildren—since I shall have none of my own—will lay aside the deference due to my antiquity, and meet me mind to mind. You say that girls are less well-mannered than of yore; but will you please recall a page in the diary of Louisa Gurney—such a well brought up little Quakeress!— which illustrates the youthful point of view:

> I was in a very playing mood today, and thoroughly enjoyed being foolish, and tried to be as rude to everybody as I could. We went on the highroad for the purpose of being rude to the folks that passed. I do think being rude is most pleasant sometimes.

One hundred and twenty-five years, Jane dear, since those illuminating sentences were penned. Now, don't write me any more lamentations over the falling off of boys and girls from heights they never attained. I only wish you had a daughter to inherit your curly hair—what good is curly hair to a son!—and your waywardness. She would be on easier—and safer—terms with you than we ever were with our mothers, she would remind you occasionally of your own "playing moods," and she would make you understand, as I can never do, the mutable qualities of youth.

Your most loving friend,
Agatha Reynolds.

Part III

Drugs and a Tense Society

Drugs and a Tense Society

Americans always consumed a great variety and quantity of alcoholic beverages, but never made drug abuse socially tolerable. The long temperance crusade, culminating in national prohibition in 1920, combined with social stigma to inhibit discussion of drug problems. But beneath the respectable surface of life in the latter part of the century, there were signs that addiction to drugs and alcohol was increasing. Every town had secret addicts, just as it had secret drinkers. Sensational newspapers and occasional political reformers exposed the evils of a hidden opium den, or the use of drugs in a red-light district. And advertisements in the best magazines and newspapers for sanatorium "cures" indicated substantial alcohol and drug abuse.

Many things combined to make drug addiction and experimentation easier than ever before. The overworked medical profession prescribed opiates and sedatives too liberally. They seemed to be wonder drugs, especially useful in combatting the growing number of cases of vague depression or tension, which doctors were poorly prepared to treat. The unregulated patent medicine industry placed a huge volume of habit-forming nostrums within the reach of nearly every family. Self-doctoring, especially in rural areas where doctors were scarce, contributed to experimentation and the chances of dependence. Technology contributed the hypodermic needle to replace the awkward opium pipe, and a host of new chemical compounds in convenient tablet or liquid form.

There was always discussion of drug addiction and misuse in the newspapers, and especially in medical journals. But by the turn of the century, press reportage and official alarm created substantial public concern. Many commentators noted the alleged widespread use of drugs among American soldiers in the Philippines after 1898. Young people were supposedly open to experimentation with drugs. And the problem surfaced dramatically in slum areas of the new cities.

Public concern peaked about the time of the First World War, and produced restraint on several levels. New local licensing and inspection laws made it harder to obtain drugs without a genuine prescription. The medical profession became better informed and was less lenient in dispensing certain drugs. Various federal statutes, especially the Harrison Act of 1914, provided closer control of drug dealers. The major powers joined in a series of Opium Conferences in 1909, 1913, and 1914, to combat production and smuggling. And the world's police bureaus cooperated through special agencies against the traffic.

These and other actions helped reduce the sense of crisis, but did not eliminate drug addition. Social disapproval remained the chief inhibition to drug abuse, and no glamor was attached to the use of drugs as part of a subculture. Addiction to hard drugs probably did not grow as fast as the population, but society continued to use lesser anodynes to cope with the unexpected tensions of modern life.

Chapter 6

How the Opium Habit
is Acquired

Virgil G. Eaton

I am not one of the persons who raise a great cry about the evils of the "opium habit." I have no doubt that the continued use of narcotics, whether they be tobacco or opium, is injurious to the nervous system; but I also firmly believe that the recuperative powers of the body are such that they can largely overcome any harmful results coming from the regular use of these substances. For instance, I know a stonecutter who resides at Cape Elizabeth, Me., who for the past twenty years has used twenty cents' worth of black "navy plug" tobacco every day. He is a large, vigorous man, weighing over two hundred pounds. His appetite is good; he sleeps well, and, save for a little heart disturbance caused by over-stimulation, he is perfectly healthy, and is likely to live until he is fourscore. He is now fifty-one years of age, and he assures me he has used tobacco since he was fourteen, and never had a fit of "swearing off" in his life. A peculiar and, I should say, a rather

Reprinted from Virgil G. Eaton, "How the Opium Habit is Acquired," in *Popular Science Monthly*, 33 (September, 1888), 663–667.

troublesome habit of his, is to go to bed every night with a big "quid" of hard "plug" tobacco between his molars. As this is always gone in the morning, and the pillow shows no traces of the weed, he thinks he chews it and swallows it in his sleep, though he never knows anything about the process.

There is a widow who keeps a lodging house in Oak Street, Boston, Mass., who takes three drachmas of morphia sulphate every day, in three one-drachma doses, morning, noon, and night. When it is remembered that an eighth of a grain is the usual dose for an adult, while two grains are sufficient to kill a man, the amount she takes seems startling. I asked her why she did not try and substitute tobacco, or bromide, or chloral hydrate for morphine, and she said they made her sick, so she could not use them. This woman is sixty years old, very pale and emaciated. Her appetite is poor. She attends to her duties faithfully, however, and is able, with the help of a girl, to carry on a large lodging house.

I might give scores of instances similar to the above, but these will do for my purpose. I believe that the person who takes liquor or tobacco or opium, in regular quantities at stated intervals, is able to withstand their effect after getting fixed in the habit, and that it is the irregular, spasmodic use of these articles which brings delirium and death. It is the man who goes on a "spree," and then quits for a time, who has the weak stomach and aching head. His neighbor, who takes his regular toddy and has his usual smoke, feels no inconvenience.

For the past year or more I have studied the growth of the opium habit in Boston. It is increasing rapidly. Not only are there more Chinese "joints" and respectable resorts kept by Americans than there were a year ago, but the number of individuals who "hit the pipe" at home and in their offices is growing very fast. A whole opium "layout," including pipe, fork, lamp, and spoon, can now be had for less than five dollars. This affords a chance for those who have acquired the habit to follow their desires in private, without having to reveal their secret to any one. How largely this is practiced I do not know, but, judging from the telltale pallor of the faces I see, I feel sure the habit is claiming more slaves every day.

In order to approximate to the amount of opium in its various forms which is used in Boston, I have made a thorough scrutiny of the physicians' recipes left at the drugstores to be filled. As is well known, all recipes given by physicians are numbered, dated, and kept on file at the drugstores, so that they may be referred to at any time. To these I went in search of information.

I was surprised to learn how extensively opium and its alkaloids —particularly sulphate of morphia—are used by physicians. I found them prescribed for every ailment which flesh is heir to. They are used for headache, sore eyes, toothache, sore throat, laryngitis, diphtheria, bronchitis, congestion, pneumonia, consumption, gastritis, liver complaint, stone in the gall-duct, carditis, aneurism, hypertrophy, peritonitis, calculus, kidney trouble, rheumatism, neuralgia, and all general or special maladies of the body. It is the great panacea and cure-all.

During my leisure time I have looked up more than 10,000 recipes. It has been my practice to go to the files, open the book, or take up a spindle at random, and take 300 recipes just as they come. The first store I visited I found 42 recipes which contained morphine out of the 300 examined. Close by, a smaller store, patronized by poorer people, had 36. Up in the aristocratic quarters, where the customers call in carriages, I found 49 morphine recipes in looking over 300. At the North End, among the poor Italian laborers, the lowest proportion of 32 in 300 was discovered. Without detailing all the places visited, I will summarize by saying that, in 10,200 recipes taken in 34 drugstores, I found 1,481 recipes which prescribed some preparation of opium, or an average of fourteen and one-half percent of the whole.

This was surprising enough; but my investigations did not end here. Of the prescriptions furnished by physicians I found that forty-two percent were filled the second time, and of those refilled twenty-three percent contained opium in some form. Again, twenty-eight percent of all prescriptions are filled a third time; and of these, sixty-one precent were for opiates; while of the twenty percent taken for the fourth filling, seventy-eight percent were for the narcotic drug, proving, beyond a doubt, that it was the opiate qualities of the medicine that afforded relief and caused the renewal.

From conversation with the druggists, I learned that the proprietary or "patent" medicines which have the largest sales were those containing opiates. One apothecary told me of an old lady who formerly came to him as often as four times a week and purchased a fifty-cent bottle of "cough-balsam." She informed him that it "quieted her nerves" and afforded rest when everything else had failed. After she had made her regular visits for over a year, he told her one day that he had sold out of the medicine required, and suggested a substitute, which was a preparation containing about the same amount of morphine. On trial, the woman found the new mixture answered every purpose of the old. The druggist then told her she had acquired the morphine habit, and from that time on she was a constant morphine user.

It was hard to learn just what proportion of those who began by taking medicines containing opiates became addicted to the habit. I should say, from what I learned, that the number was fully twenty-five percent—perhaps more. The proportion of those who, having taken up the habit in earnest, left it off later on, was very small—not over ten percent. When a person once becomes an opium slave, the habit usually holds through life.

I was told many stories about the injurious effects of morphine and opium upon the morals of those who use it. One peculiarity of a majority is that, whenever a confirmed user of the narcotic obtains credit at the drugstore, he at once stops trading at that place and goes elsewhere. All the druggists know this habit very well, and take pains to guard against it. Whenever a customer asks for credit for a bottle of morphine, the druggist informs him that the store never trusts any one; but if he has no money with him the druggist will gladly give him enough to last a day or two. In this way the druggist keeps his customer, whereas he would have lost his trade if the present had not been made at the time credit was refused.

Of course, I heard much about the irresistible desire which confirmed slaves to the habit have for their delight. There is nothing too degrading for them to do in order to obtain the narcotic. Many druggists firmly believe that a majority of the seemingly motiveless crimes which are perpetrated by reputable people are due to this habit. In pursuit of opium the slaves will resort to every trick and art which human ingenuity can invent. There is a prisoner now confined in the Concord (Mass.) Reformatory who has his opium smuggled in to him in the shape of English walnuts donated by a friend. The friend buys the opium and, opening the walnut-shells, extracts the meat, and fills up the spaces with the gum. Then he sticks the shells together with glue and sends them to the prison.

At present our clergymen, physicians, and reformers are asking for more stringent laws against the sale of these narcotics. The law compelling every person who purchases opium or other poisons to "register," giving his name and place of residence to the druggist, has been in force in Massachusetts for several years, and all this time the sales have increased. No registration law can control the traffic.

The parties who are responsible for the increase of the habit are the physicians who give the prescriptions. In these days of great mental strain, when men take their business home with them and think of it from waking to sleeping, the nerves are the first to feel the effects of overwork. Opium effects immediate relief, and the doctors, knowing this, and wishing to stand well with their patients, prescribe it more and more. Their design is to effect a cure. The result is to convert their patients into opium slaves. The doctors are to blame for so large a consumption of opium, and they are the men who need reforming.

Two means of preventing the spread of the habit suggest themselves to every thoughtful person:

1. Pass a law that no prescriptions containing opium or its preparations can be filled more than once at the druggist's without having the physician renew it. The extra cost of calling on a doctor when the medicine ran out would deter many poor people from acquiring the habit. Such a law would also make the doctors more guarded in prescribing opiates for trivial ailments. With the law in force, and the druggists guarded by strict registration laws, we could soon trace the responsibility to its proper source, and then, if these safeguards were not enough, physicians could be fined for administering opiates save in exceptional cases.

2. The great preventive to the habit is to keep the body in such a state that it will not require sedatives or stimulants. The young men and women in our cities have too big heads, too small necks, and too flabby muscles. They should forsake medicine, and patronize the gymnasium. Let them develop their muscles and rest their nerves, and the family doctor, who means well, but who can not resist the tendency of the age, can take a protracted vacation. Unless something of the kind is done soon, the residents of our American cities will be all opium slaves.

Chapter 7

Narcotic Addiction

Perry M. Lichtenstein, M. D.

The subject of narcotic addiction is now receiving the attention that it deserves. When we note the number of young men and women in our prisons subject to this terrible curse, and study their marked physical and moral degenerative changes, we awake to the fact that we must stop the growth of this habit if we wish to save future generations. This article is based upon the observation and treatment of 1,000 cases within the City Prison in Manhattan, during one year's service. The average number of prisoners admitted in one year is 16,000, making the percentage of narcotic habitués, therefore, five percent. The increase in the number of people addicted to habit-forming drugs has been extraordinary within the last five years. The greatest increase has been within the last year. Whether or not this is due to a natural increase in the number of people addicted is difficult to say; it may be due to the enforcement of the laws relative to the use of narcotics, thus bringing a greater number to our attention. I am inclined to believe the

Excerpted from Perry M. Lichtenstein, M. D., "Narcotic Addiction," in *New York Medical Journal,* 100 (November 14, 1914), 962–966.

former; for when one notes the number of young prisoners addicted to the use of drugs, and takes into consideration the period of addiction, it is easy to see that habit formation is on the increase.

As regards the acquisition of the habit, I have ascertained the following: The number of victims who directly trace their addiction to physicians' prescriptions is very small; I have found but twenty such people out of 1,000. Most of these victims were women who had been suffering from tubal disease. One woman had been severely burned and had to be given opiates to quiet her. The information given by physicians to patients, that they had been receiving morphine, cocaine, etc., is to be deplored. Patients should be kept in ignorance as to medication. Other prisoners have stated that they had been induced by friends to take a "sniff" of the drug, which is variously termed "happy dust," "snow," etc.

Several individuals have come to the conclusion that selling "dope" is a very profitable business. These individuals have sent their agents among the gangs frequenting our city corners, instructing them to make friends with the members and induce them to take the drug. Janitors, bartenders, and cabmen have also been employed to help spread the habit. The plan has worked so well that there is scarcely a poolroom in New York that may not be called a meeting place of drug fiends. The drug has been made up in candy and sold to school children. The conspiring individuals, being familiar with the habit-forming action of the drugs, believe that the increased number of "fiends" will create a larger demand for the drug, and in this way build up a profitable business.

Many individuals begin taking a narcotic for insomnia; this is particularly true of physicians and nurses. I have treated many nurses addicted to morphine taken hypodermically. Others take the drug to ward off sorrow and care, and still others are compelled to take the drug because of severe pains caused by locomotor ataxia, cancer, etc. The number of young people addicted is enormous. I have come in contact with individuals sixteen and eighteen years of age, whose history was that they had taken a habit-forming drug for at least two years. This includes girls as well as boys.

When once the drug has taken hold on these people, they will do anything to acquire a supply. The charges against dope fiends are usually petty crimes; they steal just enough to enable them to obtain a supply of the drug. Once in prison they will try every-thing and anything to obtain the drug. During my experience with habitués in the City Prison, I have witnessed many ways in which the attempt to smuggle in the drug has been made. On one occa-sion, a can of condensed milk was sent to a "fiend." The can did not show signs of having been tampered with. On prying off the lid, the searcher found a finger cot full of morphine in the milk, and a note to the effect that more was coming. On another occa-sion a package of cigarettes was sent to a prisoner; the government seal was unbroken. When opened, the cigarettes were found wrapped in silver leaf and upon examination proved to be loaded with morphine tablets. On another occasion two books were sent to an habitué. The searcher noticed a white powder on his desk. He opened the book, but could find no trace of a drug. He slit open the binding and found two packages, one containing morphine and the other heroin. On still another occasion a magazine was sent in, which upon examination by the warden disclosed a picture pasted on one of the pages, under which picture a large amount of morphine was secreted. The ways in which drug smuggling is attempted are too numerous to mention in this paper.

It is necessary to define the action of opium and its derivatives, also that of cocaine, in order to understand the effect of these drugs upon habitués. I will confine myself to the actions on the nervous system, it being obvious that habitués take drugs for this purpose only. Opium causes an increase in intellectual powers and stimulates the imagination. External occurrences seem to have no effect upon the individual. The imagination is usually pleasantly excited. All cares and sorrow are forgotten, and the subject feels content and happy. This is followed by a dreamy state, due to the suppression of external stimuli and the depressant effect upon all centres, resulting in sleep. The person has fantastic dreams, often of an impossible nature. The period of narcosis is deep and the patient is not easily aroused. The pupils are contracted and react sluggishly to light. All reflexes, excepting the pupillary, are first stimulated and then depressed.

After the cessation of the action, the patient is restless, dull, repulsive, and unable to concentrate his thoughts. Perversion of the moral feelings is a marked mental symptom. Delusions of persecution may occur and some prisoners show marked hallucinatory excitement. The reflexes are exaggerated owing to the removal of the depressing action of the drug upon the spinal cord. The action of cocaine differs from that of morphine. All the mental faculties are stimulated by this drug and the subject has a great increase of bodily power. One man stated that it was a common occurrence for him to go seventy-two hours without sleep, while under the influence of this drug. At the end of that time he collapsed and had to take more of the drug in order to brace himself. All care and sorrow are forgotten and the person is supremely happy. The stimulating effect of cocaine is followed by physical and mental exhaustion, enfeeblement of the intellect, and headaches. Cocaine causes a dilation of the pupil from action upon the sympathetic. Habitués, when in need of the drug, frequently complain of a feeling of foreign bodies crawling under the skin. During the stage of stimulation the reflexes are exaggerated. The depressive stage is accompanied by decreased activity of reflexes. The pupils react to light, but not very well to accommodation.

Many people are of the opinion that all habitués are emaciated, sallow looking, bleary eyed individuals, who take no interest in anything. This is not so. Not all drunkards are red faced, red nosed, and shabby looking. The drunkard on the Bowery is a different looking individual from the drunkard on Fifth Avenue. The same is true of drug habitués. The drug fiend who hangs out in poolrooms and "hop joints," who has no particular occupation, and gets about one square meal a week will look different from, and not last as long as the one who has fine surroundings, three square meals a day, and an occupation. True, he may not attend to business as strictly as he should, nevertheless, his associations make it imperative to confine himself to a certain period of the day in taking the drug. I have come in contact with individuals who had been addicted to a habit-forming drug for twenty-five years and still looked well nourished. People who take the drug as previously described, i.e., under unfavorable conditions, usually present a sallow, haggard appearance; they look as if they had lost all interest in the world. The eyes are dull, and the individual can concentrate his mind only on one thought, i.e., how to obtain the drug. If the drug is not given, they show what are known as withdrawal symptoms. The habitué complains of abdominal pains, severe cramps in the legs and arms, and precordial pains. He presents an appearance which once noted is never forgotten.

•   •   •

As to addiction among the different races, I may state that in proportion to the number of prisoners of each race admitted, I have reached the following conclusions:

1. Yellow race: Most frequently addicted; opium smokers and opium and yen shi chewers; rarely take cocaine and rarely use the hypodermic syringe.

2. Black race: Cocaine users, particularly those coming from our Southern States; also smoke opium and use heroin, the latter not as frequently, however, as the white race.

3. White race: Heroin, morphine, and cocaine users; frequent users of the hypodermic syringe; also smoke opium, but not as frequently as the Chinese.

It is rare to see a colored or a Chinese hypodermic fiend. White women, when once addicted to drugs, very frequently resort to the hypodermic syringe. As to sex, the male habitués greatly outnumber the female.

It is interesting to note the nationalities, occupations, and social standing of those addicted. The Chinese, American, and Italian, in the order named, are the three nationalities most frequently represented, taking those admitted to our prisons as a standard. The Hebrew American is very frequently addicted. In all my experience I have had only one Greek who took morphine. Greeks, as well as Syrians, Turks, Swedes, and Norwegians are seldom addicted. Russians and Germans, recent residents of this country, are seldom among those habituated.

As regards occupation, the cases observed and treated by me showed that the employment of habitués required little effort and gave them plenty of leisure time. The occupations given were as follows in the order named: Salesmen, clerks, newsdealers, truck drivers, actors, stenographers, waiters and waitresses, and cooks. I have found very few who gave a history of performing very laborious work.

Among the women, in the order named, the occupations were actresses, nurses, and saleswomen. Most of these had been arrested for soliciting, keeping disorderly houses, or shoplifting. The social standing of habitués is an interesting item. The greater number are of the gangster type and consequently are mental and moral degenerates. It is surprising, however, to learn how many habitués are of the better class. Physicians, nurses, and actresses, also some of the very richest of our people, frequently have elaborate "layouts" in their homes, richly furnished, and stocked with the handsomest jeweled opium pipes. Many of these people naturally never attract our attention because of the absence of marked physical changes, due to good surroundings, good meals, etc.

To repeat, we must stop drug habit formation. The rapid growth of this habit threatens to dwarf alcoholic addiction. As we know the terrible effects of these drugs, the ultimate results may readily be foreseen.

●   ●   ●

Chapter 8

Morphinism and Crime

L. L. Stanley

Within the past three years, at San Quentin penitentiary, over 100 prisoners have been received who admitted verbally or by their actions that they were confirmed addicts to opium in some of its forms. As soon as these addicts are received at the prison they are measured and photographed according to the Bertillon system, and are then turned over to the medical deparment for examination and treatment. Most of these men have just come from the various county jails where they had their potion, which usually suffices them until they reach the penitentiary. By this time the so-called "habit" is coming on and the habitué is a pitiable sight. After obtaining from the patient his method of administration and the amount he usually takes, the required dose to ease him is given, and soon his normal attitude and behavior returns.

It is at this time that information regarding his addiction and its relation to crime, in greater detail, is brought from him. All of his

Excerpted from L. L. Stanley, "Morphinism and Crime," in *Journal of the American Institute of Criminal Law and Criminology,* 8 (January, 1918), 749–756. Reprinted by special permission of the American Institute of Criminal Law and Criminology (Northwestern University School of Law), Volume 8, No. 5, 1918.

answers to the questions asked him are carefully written down, and later tabulated and studied with the purpose in view of learning more about this dreadful affliction.

One of the first questions asked is as to the age at which he commenced the use of "dope." Of the one hundred so questioned:

> One, or 1%, began at eight years;
> One, or 1% began at thirteen years;
> One, or 1%, began at fourteen years;
> Three, or 3%, began at fifteen years.

It is seen that approximately six percent began when they were mere children, before they had completed the grammar grades.

> Eight commenced at sixteen years;
> Six commenced at seventeen years;
> Fourteen commenced at eighteen years;
> Nine commenced at nineteen years;
> Eight commenced at twenty years.

Forty-eight began the use of "dope" between the ages of fifteen and twenty-one years. Including the three who commenced before fifteen years it is shown that fifty-one percent or over one-half of the addictions of this series are formed before the youth reached his majority.

> Five began at twenty-one years;
> Five began at twenty-two years;
> Eight began at twenty-three years;
> Four began at twenty-four years;
> Two began at twenty-five years.

Thus in early manhood, between twenty-one and twenty-five years, twenty-four first succumbed to this evil.

From twenty-five to thirty years twelve began its use, and in the next decade, from thirty to forty years, a like number. After the age of forty, no addiction were formed in this series of cases.

It is seen by these figures that morphinism is usually acquired before the youth is normally away from the guardianship of his parents, and at a time when he should be guided by better influences. It is the time when his mind is relatively plastic and easily moulded.

The second question asked is: "What kind did you use first?" In answer to this, it was learned that fifty-eight began by smoking opium, twenty percent used morphine hypodermically, eight ate morphine, three ate "yen shee," the ashes of opium, and the remaining cases started by using cocaine and laudanum, or eating opium. This shows that the greatest danger lies in the smoking of opium, for most commence in this way.

Contrast to this, the answers to the questions as to the kind they used last:

Forty-eight use morphine by syringe;

Eight take morphine by mouth;

Twenty-eight percent use both morphine and cocaine;

Three still smoke opium.

Others use morphine by mouth and syringe together, according to circumstances, while some take heroin and laudanum. In fact, after the habit is well formed, an addict will take anything he can get his hands on.

This shows that although the majority started their addiction by smoking opium, they subsequently changed to using morphine by the hypodermic syringe.

Of course, it is difficult to obtain accurate statements from the addicts as to the amount of drug they use. Some do not know the quantity they take and others use as much as they can secure.

Eighteen percent admit less than five grains a day;

Thirty-two percent admit five to ten grains a day;

Thirty-two percent admit ten to twenty grains a day;

Six percent admit twenty to thirty grains a day;

Six percent admit thirty to forty grains a day.

Four percent claim to use over sixty grains a day, when they can obtain it. When it is realized that one-fourth grain is the adult dosage, it is seen how a tolerance for the drug may be created, and what enormous amounts may be taken without fatal results.

A natural inquiry has reference to the occupation engaged in by these persons when they began their addiction. Of the one hundred, seven each were waiters and sailors, six were tailors, five each were messenger boys, porters and laborers, while four each were showmen, racetrack followers, prisoners, teamsters, and schoolboys. Bartenders, gamblers, bookkeepers, cooks, and idlers numbered three each. This is as to be expected—seamen, adventurers, actors, gamblers, racetrack followers—for the most part, the lower stratum of society. Waiters, tailors, and men of like occupations, after a hard day's work, seek relaxation in the peaceful pipe with their associates of like inclinations.

Knowing the relatively tender ages at which this habit is

formed, it is of interest to find out just how the use of dope was begun. To this question there were a great many answers.

Fifty, or one-half, began by associating with bad companions at night, frequenting dance halls, saloons, poolrooms, and later "joints," where they were induced to try the pipe. Very few who ever try the pipe have willpower enough to refrain from doing the same thing again at some future date when they are importuned to do so by their evil associates. Fifteen percent were induced and educated to this addiction by women of the underworld, who perhaps took a fancy to the young man and persuaded him to go with her to indulge in this insidious vice. Eleven claim that they learned to smoke opium in jails and penitentiaries.

In the not far remote periods of the two California penitentiaries it was not difficult to have opium smuggled inside the walls, where men not cured of their addiction would use the drug and induce younger prisoners to be "sports and take a shot." At the present time, however, a close watch is kept at the prisons and no contraband is allowed to enter. But at the county jails no such rigid vigilance is in force, and it is said by the prisoners who have come from those jails, that it is a very easy matter for any one who has money to have the drug brought to him. It is in those jails that many a young man is induced to become an addict to this habit because he wishes to show his toughened cell mates that he can be as bad a man as any of them.

Sixteen others claim that they began the use of dope on account of various sicknesses, such as rheumatism, accidents, syphilis and other forms of disease in which there was a high degree of pain. In some of these cases, it might have been the fault of the physician or of the nurse that the patient found out what he was receiving for his pain and in this way led him on to his addiction.

One patient examined at San Quentin began by taking paregoric for stomachache, with which he was troubled to a considerable extent. He was given this by his mother when he was at the age of seven years. From this frequent dosage he acquired the habit, the persistence in which finally landed him in jail. A second addict stated that when he was in high school in a certain town in Nevada, it was a fad among the boy and girl students to visit Chinatown regularly, where they smoked opium. Another told that while in the Alaskan fisheries, he, with a number of other men, was given morphine to stimulate him to greater efforts and to work at higher tension so that all of the fish might be taken care of in a limited time without pecuniary loss to the company. At the end of the season, he was, with a number of other men, a confirmed addict.

Messenger boys in large cities are especially susceptible to falling into this habit. One of their chief means of income is derived from female outcasts of the underworld, who send them to obtain the drug. With these associates it is not difficult to be led to the addiction.

The longest period over which any of the hundred had been using morphine was thirty years, and the shortest was eighteen months, with an average of thirteen years.

•   •   •

Considering the foregoing phases of the "dope" question, there is no doubt that opium plays a great part in crime. It is safe to say, that if opium did not have its habit-forming properties, there would be at least two percent fewer criminals in our institutions, for of all the addicts examined, none laid the cause of his crime to anything other than "dope."

The greater number of felonies committed by "drug habitués" are robbery or grand larceny. It is when the habit is coming on with all its attendant misery that the "fiend" goes forth to procure his drug at whatever cost. They have no fear; only one object in view—"relief."

One colored addict accompanied by a female consort, herself also a user, stole a motorcycle in one town and wheeled it to another town five miles away, where they tried to sell it in order to purchase opium. Another addict is now serving a sentence for peddling "dope." He was a higher-up, and had many under him who disposed of the drug which he procured. He states that many of his former associates are now behind the bars.

One-half hour after having taken twelve grains of morphine, one fiend walked into the front door of a private residence in the day time, and stole jewelry and money.

A tailor, aged twenty-three, burglarized a drug store from which he took the total supply of morphine, and five hundred dollars besides.

Another "hop head," loaded with morphine, went into a room, and "frisked" the sleeping occupant's clothes of six dollars and a half.

One other addict entered a house, which was being newly furnished, and stole the new carpet, making three trips into the house to complete the operation.

Another is serving a sentence for pimping. He says that if it had not been for morphine, he would not have been pimping. His consort taught him the morphine habit.

Still another, in need of morphine, passed one-cent pieces of old coinage for ten dollar gold coins. In many cases he was successful. Opium led him into crime once before when he was sentenced to prison for pocket picking.

One other who was a "twilight prowler" is now serving his third term in prison. "Had it not been for dope," he said, "I would never have been a thief."

Part IV

The Industrial Environment

The Industrial Environment

The effort to conserve America's natural resources was a major goal of the progressive era. Reaction to the effects of industrialism on the general environment was less publicized. The problems involved were scientifically complex, even to the few available experts. But those citizens, usually in cities, directly affected were quick to seek solutions. Their responses, and the ways in which they viewed the environment, revealed how deeply American ideals and tastes conflicted with the need to oversee industrialism.

City governments reacted first to new environmental problems. Officials quickly learned to secure, treat, store, and deliver huge quantities of water. But their chief aim was pure drinking water. People seldom conceived of a water shortage which technology could not correct. Only a few scientific experts perceived the ill effects of water pollutants on marine life.

Progress in sewerage paralleled developments in water technology, but despite great advances only a small part of the country's sewage passed through more than minimal treatment. The taxpayers' reluctance to accept increased tax rates often forced public officials to find cheaper methods. The ultimate aim was usually to dump sewage into large bodies of water, where tides and natural cleansing actions supposedly made wastes harmless.

Pure air was also a major goal of urban technicians. The effect of soot, fumes, and ashes on health was clear to doctors and scientists, but to most citizens dirty air was "the smoke nuisance." It ruined wash on the lines, dirtied collars, and smarted the eyes. Technology to eliminate some heavy smoke was available, and many citizens groups attacked the problem in the name of civic improvement and beautification. But that same smoke signalled prosperity and full employment to other boosters, eager to use it as a sign of their community's wealth.

Garbage disposal was probably the major unexpected result of urbanization and growing affluence. Small town authorities provided a dump or incinerator, but managers of large cities developed more sophisticated measures. Sanitation workers used technology and ingenuity to sort and recycle some garbage. Paper, rags, bottles, heavy metals were reused; food scraps became animal feed. Economics rather than any concept of recycling or scarcity, however, prompted this. Mass production techniques had not yet made consumer goods cheap enough to be used once and then disposed as litter. Much of the treated garbage went to landfills, which became progressively expensive to maintain. The rest went to the incinerator, often to be dumped in a river or at sea as "purified ashes." As was so often the case, every progressive innovation or technique dealing with the environment seemed to produce unpredicted side effects.

The effort to provide new "services" to city dwellers incidentally helped control environmental damage, but was often full of ironies. The horses that did most of society's brute labor, for instance, were the most obvious polluters of any street. Small wonder that many observers welcomed the automobile as a deliverance from horse manure. The internal combustion engine did not seem a pollution threat. In the meantime, city officials greatly increased the number of street sweepers who cleaned up after horses, and employed new high-pressure washing techniques to clean streets of manure. Of course, these processes simply flushed huge quantities of untreated animal waste into the nearest river or bay.

Electricity was the power of the future—safe, clean, and efficient. It would eliminate smoking trains, belching smokestacks; transform the kitchen, and rid the home of oil or coal heating; and eliminate dirt, noise, and bad air. Few observers saw that in the absence of falling water, huge quantities of fossil fuels would be needed to generate electricity. Fewer still foresaw a waste of energy in gadgets; or a whole new category of pollution that came with power lines and poles.

The relation of population growth to waste and pollution was also vague. Most commentators believed that western man's population growth was slowing, and nations like France and Britain feared "race suicide." President Theodore Roosevelt was especially insistent on the duty to reproduce, and gave special awards to parents of large families. Some commentators argued otherwise, but few Americans believed the country would become overcrowded. And science was steadily offering means to improve crop yields and cultivate marginal lands. Many people responded to conservationists' efforts to save topsoil, protect wildlife, and preserve wilderness areas; but few believed that the earth's resources were intrinsically limited.

The first generation of Americans to live with burgeoning industrialism and its social effects faced new and puzzling environmental problems. They responded quickly and optimistically, believing in the generally progressive nature of technology. In a purely technical sense—controlling water, sewage, and garbage—they were successful. And while there was a developing environmental problem, the sheer scope of America inhibited any sense of crisis.

The most disturbing result of the generation's response to the environmental question was not technical weakness, but the failure to alter attitudes that promoted waste and inhibited planning. Americans traditionally alternated between the desire to subdue nature, and the urge to return to its pristine qualities. It was difficult for them to accept legal controls on individuals. The conflicting jurisdictions of the federal system and political dealing also allowed major interests to avoid serious regulation.

But in the end, a general attitude probably most inhibited efforts to control environmental development. America rested on the idea of abundance. The possibility of obtaining affluence underlay the general adherence to individualism, and the aversion to governmental planning. To concede or accept the idea of ultimate scarcity would require a reevaluation of the national ethic.

Environmental problems seemed new, susceptible to technical solutions, and the era had almost unlimited faith in problem solving over general regulation. But industrialism and the tastes it created never lacked critics, who built a legacy for the future.

Chapter 9

Smoke Abatement in Cincinnati

Matthew Nelson

I much regret that it should be so, but the visitors to our city today will have the fact impressed upon their minds that Cincinnati is neither a "smokeless" nor a "spotless" town. Nevertheless, had they been here two years ago they would undoubtedly now admit that some good work has been done in the elimination of smoke from many of the Cincinnati stacks. Nature has been overwhelmingly considerate to some cities in giving them waterfalls for power purposes, whilst we have to be thankful for bituminous coal. I rejoice to say, however, that even if it prove only a temporary substitute, we have been using natural gas for about two months with the most desirable results, and the demand of merchants and manufacturers for it is increasing rapidly. The Gibson House Hotel whose stack is directly opposite the Sinton, together with the Havlin Hotel two blocks away and the Burnet House close by, are now smokeless, although at one time the emanations of smoke from them presented one of the greatest nuisances in the

Reprinted From Matthew Nelson, "Smoke Abatement in Cincinnati," in *American City,* 2 (January, 1910), 8–10.

city. The former hostelry was one of the first to use natural gas. Sincerely do I trust that the price of the material may not prove prohibitive, and that the supply will be inexhaustible.

The large Power Building at Eighth and Sycamore for the past year has been a standing monument of what a good appliance and careful firing will do. The stack has been and *is* absolutely smokeless, and the saving in coal bills has been over twenty-five percent. What between its factory stacks and the locomotives Eggleston Avenue two years ago was one of the dirtiest and most disagreeable districts in the city. Next time you are passing glance down it. Although there are some twenty stacks along that avenue, I believe nearly all are smokeless.

Many of our East End residents have doubtless observed the conduct of the Traction Company's stacks at Pendleton, and I think they must admit, that for a plant of its size, the stacks are doing most excellent work. In fact they too are almost smokeless. I wish I could say the same with regard to our new waterwork's plant at the foot of Torrence Road.

One day last week I happened to be in one of the most smoky districts in the city watching two stacks, the owners of which I arrested a month ago. In my line of view I counted nearly forty stacks, the two to which I refer being the only smokers. It is needless to say that I was much pleased on observing this improvement.

We should have much more cooperation in our work from the architects than we are receiving. Some of these gentlemen are either extremely ignorant on the subject of furnaces and boilers and how they should be built and set, or they are wilfully ignoring the scientific laws of construction and consistent boiler settings. For example: our newly erected skyscraper at Seventh and Vine has its furnaces and stokers under the sidewalk on Seventh Street, and instead of the smokestack being erected right over these, it was placed at the far end of the building, sixty feet away, necessitating, of course, an immense breaching of the same number of feet in length to convey the smoke to the stack. Do you wonder that this magnificent new building has added one more smoky chimney to our city? So long as plants are built in this manner we shall have smoky stacks, and this notwithstanding the fact, clearly established, that bituminous coal high in volatile matter can be burned with economy and absolutely without smoke. Plants having faulty furnaces and improperly set boilers are only able to operate up to about one-half, and never over three-fourths of their efficiency.

If merchants or manufacturers who contemplate the erection of new buildings, or the making of alterations in their furnaces would submit their plans and specifications to the Smoke Abatement League *before they are signed up,* its officials will be more than pleased to give them, free of any charges, some very valuable information which may save them a great deal of money by having their furnaces properly constructed before they are fired. The great lesson to be learned here is to build the furnace so that the flame and the distilled gases shall not be allowed to come into contact with the boiler surfaces until combustion is complete. This lesson, however, can never be learned when boilers are set only twenty inches above the grate bars. On top of these grates a fire six or eight inches deep must be placed, leaving but fourteen or twelve inches clear space to the boiler. This is a condition which can produce nothing but smoke and a waste of greenbacks.

Locomotives have received as much attention as it is possible to bestow upon them with the two assistants I have, and I am glad to be able to announce to this meeting that the Pennsylvania Railroad informs me that every switch engine in their yards in Cincinnati has steam jets attached. This sounds lovely, but alas! like their brothers in manufacturing plans, the railroad engineer and fireman find it too much trouble to give the necessary half turn of the wrist to set the jet going; and many locomotives are consequently sending forth dense volumes of black smoke infinitely worse than those emanating from the stacks of large factories. Perhaps if the city ordinance was amended to give the City Smoke Inspector and his deputies the power of arrest, so that crews of locomotives could be taken off their engines, and their trains could be stopped for violating the smoke ordinance, it might have a very wholesome effect.

The problem of smoke abatement evidently resolves itself into the problem of the production of perfect combusion. Probably twice as much coal is used in boiler furnaces, and six times as much in domestic fires as is theoretically required for the production of the effects obtained. Of course, much of this enormous waste could be prevented by improved methods of combustion, which would solve the smoke problem. Naturally, dwellings greatly outnumber factories, and are partly responsible for the smoky condition of the atmosphere; but we have so many factories in this city, not to mention locomotives, to which our attention must be given, that we are not quite prepared to take the question of dwellings into consideration except in very chronic cases.

The evil effects of town air on plant life and human lungs, often attributed to preventable smoke, are in reality due to the non-preventable sulphuric acid as the active agent of destruction. This is produced from the coal during the process of combustion. It eats everything. Nothing escapes its voracity. It bites the bark off trees, ruins iron fencing, crumbles stone buildings, and at the present moment is eating the stonework of St. Paul and Westminster Cathedrals as well as the granite of our new skyscrapers.

It is not, of course, the business of any member of our staff personally to recommend a particular stoker, or any kind of coal to owners of plants. For obvious reasons we must not do this, but I maintain that it *is* our business to denounce any stoker, which, when it is purchased in good faith and installed, does nothing but smoke. Stokers which are sold like this particular one on a commission basis, which commission is, of course, paid by the purchaser whether he is aware of the fact or not, will never meet with the approval of the Smoke Abatement League's officials. The extreme opposite of this instrument infernal and intolerable is the stoker which is sold absolutely on its merits alone, and without the question of commission appearing at either end of the transaction. To intending purchasers a few words of warning as to the kind of stokers *not* to buy would, therefore, not be amiss. One of the very best smoke preventers known is a good fireman, but alas? if he could be anything else he would not be a fireman; hence this good and careful servant is sadly lacking where most needed.

I regret to say that some of our city buildings are bad smokers. It was doubtless for this reason that the authorities of the city appointed a City Smoke Inspector! Owing to lack of funds the Smoke Abatement League's officials made but sixteen arrests last year. Up to the first of November of the present year, however, fifty arrests have been made, and six fines of $25.00 and costs each have been imposed. A most vigorous campaign is still being carried on by the League. In fact, as Paul Jones once said, "we have just begun to fight." No one likes the introduction of an innovation, especially if it interferes with the old way of doing business dating fifty or more years back, and it is, therefore, occasionally necessary to make the arrest of a stubborn sinner in order that the Presiding Judge of the Police Court, to whom he *must* give a respectful hearing, can get a few words of wholesome advice into his ear. This gives me my opportunity, and I verily believe that at least ninety-five percent of the persons whom I have arrested are today my best friends. Why? Simply because I have been permitted to show them that I could save them money in their coal bills if they follow the advice given them.

The actual annual waste of money through, shall I say, the careless and ignorant handling of coal has been estimated at six hundred millions of dollars. As far as I can ascertain, however, this is merely a guess, and I believe the guess of an annual loss of a *billion dollars* would be much nearer the mark. Astounding figures like these should make the visit of the Smoke Inspector to a manufacturing plant an extremely pleasant one, but it is often the reverse, for he frequently is a silent listener to the anathemas hurled at his head, when he has a right to expect to be welcomed with showers of blessings.

The question of smoke abatement has now become well-nigh universal. The movement has come to stay, yet it is far from receiving the general attention it demands. Coal has, of course, its many virtues, but these are apparently counterbalanced by its greater vices, usually superinduced by the work of the inexperienced fireman or the grossly ignorant engineer. It was brought into use in London towards the end of the thirteenth century, and the smoke from it was considered so injurious to health that, during the reign of Kind Edward the First, proclamations were issued forbidding its consumption during the sitting of Parliament. In 1646 Londoners even petitioned Parliament to prohibit its injurious effect. For seven centuries, therefore, soft coal has been a most destructive element. Everything which has life, whether in earth, air or water, spends its existence and its life forces in a perpetual battle against death. Why, then, not help us to prevent coal, one of our most useful products, from becoming an auxiliary to the ever-conquering and still unconquered power of death?

Chapter 10

The Pollution of
Lakes and Rivers

We quoted not long ago from the remarks made by Mr. Roosevelt at Buffalo urging the necessity of putting a stop to the pollution of the water of the Great Lakes and declaring that civilized people ought to be able to dispose of sewage in a better way than by putting it into drinking water. The issue thus touched upon is one of prime importance in New York State. Something over a year ago Governor Hughes in a message said, "We have reached a time in the development of this state when proper measures for the protection of our streams are imperatively needed. We can no longer afford to permit the sewage of our cities and our industrial wastes to be poured into our watercourses. . . . Our present laws are inadequate and ought to be thoroughly revised." While it is true that there is some question as to whether it is possible to keep any large body of water or large river free from pollution, and whether, accordingly, the best way of dealing with the subject may not be to compel local communities to purify such water or obtain their supply from another source, yet the duty of prevent-

Reprinted from "The Pollution of Lakes and Rivers," in *The Outlook,* 96 (September 24, 1910), 144–145.

ing the pollution so far as possible is positive. The facts show that the pollution of the Niagara River and Lake Erie is frightful in its extent and that it is a national as well as a local problem. A writer in a bulletin issued by the Department of Health of New York State asserts that the town of Niagara Falls is "one of the worst plague spots, if not the very worst, in respect of typhoid fever in the United States today," and that the enormous typhoid death rate of this town is due almost wholly to the pollution of the public water by the sewage of the city of Buffalo. Other towns, such as Tonawanda, North Tonawanda, and Lockport, suffer from the same cause, and the completion in Buffalo of a new sewer system now under way will, it is alleged, increase the evil seriously.

The larger lake ports themselves undoubtedly are subject to typhoid fever and to other communicable diseases which result from an impure water supply. When it is considered that the danger extends not only to the residents of these places but to travelers on railways and on lake boats which use the impure water, and when it is remembered that over fifteen million passengers are carried yearly in boats on the Great Lakes and that over a million people a year visit Niagara Falls, it is evident that the spreading of diseases such as typhoid must exist in an appreciable degree all over the United States.

In almost every village so-called sporadic cases of typhoid appear from time to time, and how many of these may result from the pollution of the waters of the Great Lakes, Niagara River, and the Erie Canal it would be impossible to judge. Bills have been introduced in Congress as well as in the New York State Legislature to forbid the pollution, but so far nothing has been accomplished, and the cities of Lake Erie and the Niagara frontier continue to have about four hundred deaths yearly from typhoid and probably not far from four thousand cases of the disease. The mere statement of these facts is more forcible than any rhetoric. Whether the MacKenzie-Wood Bill, which would permit the State Commissioner of Health to order Buffalo, for instance, to change its system of sewerage at a cost of many million dollars, is or is not the best way of dealing with the question, is not the main problem.

What must be urged, with literally the pressure of life and death importance, is that the Legislature of New York and the municipal bodies of the cities and towns involved take up the matter instantly, actively, and efficiently. Foul water is almost, if not quite, the greatest cause of preventable diseases in this country, and as our civilization and our public intelligence grow it becomes more and more possible to wipe out of existence, or at least greatly reduce, the frightful death rate which may certainly be ascribed to this cause. It is said that pollution of water kills as many people in the United States annually as the historic Black Plagues which used to ravage the ignorant, unsanitary people of centuries ago. This reproach is one that can be and must be removed.

Chapter 11

Advertising

John Robertson

Advertising may be divided into two classes, the legitimate and the "puff." Under the first head may be included legal and business notices and mere uncolored announcements, put forth for the sole purpose of giving publicity to a certain fact. So far as these are concerned, there is little, if any, of the "humbug" element involved; and, whether such advertisements are published in the form of handbills, posters, or notices in the columns of local journals, all is comparatively straightforward and aboveboard. But how about the puffs, the puffers and the puffees? Take up a newspaper, reader—any one will do—and run your eye down the advertising column; what will be your first impression? Most probably one of bewildered admiration and regret at what may, very likely, appear to you a wasteful expenditure of ingenuity and money. But *is* it wasted? Some people may think so, but they are woefully mistaken. Experience tells a different tale. Some of the devices employed to attract attention are certainly both shallow

Reprinted from John Robertson, "Advertising," in *Appleton's Journal,* 5 (April 1, 1871), 372–373.

and transparent, yet even these will "draw" a certain class of the community. Ask a practical advertising agent, and he will tell you, almost to a fraction, what the expenditure of a specified number of dollars will bring in; and, strange to say, the larger the outlay, the greater the *percentage* of profit will be! Take, for instance, the item of patent medicines—commodities for which there would be absolutely no sale whatever without resorting to advertising. There is one firm in New England, extensively engaged in this business, the head of which began life, some forty years ago, as a poor little ragged urchin, running errands for a druggist in a provincial town in the State of Massachusetts, at the munificent salary of a dollar a week, and who at present pays more than two hundred and fifty thousand dollars per annum for newspaper advertising alone throughout the Union, and distributes, gratis, about seven million pamphlets, printed in eight different languages (Chinese included), besides handbills, etc., costing many thousand dollars more! What his profits are may be guessed from the simple but suggestive fact of his paying about fifty-six thousand dollars a year to the United States Internal Revenue for the two- and four-cent stamps affixed to the five different preparations which he offers for sale! There is one great peculiarity in advertisers of this class: *their advertising must be continuous.* It must never diminish nor be relaxed even for a day. Were there a lull or cessation in the stream in any one district, however insignificant, the result would immediately become apparent in a waning of popularity and diminished sales. A patent medicine business, accordingly, can never be properly called "established," for its existence depends solely on its being kept before the public. When advertising is discontinued, the business becomes defunct, and can rarely be resuscitated.

The enormous increase in the number of advertisements nowadays has naturally caused a deal of competition; people must keep pace with the times, and consequently brains are daily tortured and ingenuity racked to produce something original and startling to catch the public eye and tickle popular fancy. Sometimes we see a notice "set up" in the actual shape and form of the article advertised, such as a teapot or a hat; again the paragraph appears with a rough blank line drawn completely through it—an artistic idea and one which rarely failed to attract attention before it became so common. Then we have occasionally a whole column left blank, with the exception of the name and address of the advertiser with one or two of his *spécialités*. All these, however, are mere appeals to the eye; far greater variety, and even more ingenuity, is displayed in the compilation and actual wording of some of the mendacious and insinuating announcements which have a higher and bolder aim, that of directly engaging our sympathies and exciting our interest. Specious and plausible, indeed, are some of these, the two grand ideas being for the advertiser to leave no stone unturned to puff his own wares and to depreciate those of each and every one of his competitors. Articles christened after the names of celebrated or notorious characters will always command a sale for a time; dry goods going at "Tremendous sacrifices!" or "Selling under cost!" if announced in flaring capitals, will always draw crowds of ladies, while the sterner sex will offer themselves as only too willing victims at the shrine of the first new hat labelled "The Latest Parisian Novelty!"

There are many other methods of advertising—some of them even more illegitimate and objectionable. The possession of a fast horse or yacht, an exceptionally splendid equipage, a regal mansion, palatial business premises, or a lavish expenditure, have frequently proved winning cards; while sensational domestic squabbles, carefully elaborated in the public press, have been resorted to, and not unsuccessfully either, by some unscrupulous adventurers to attain the great twin object of their ambition— money and notoriety. We have poetical puffs as well; and these, although for the most part vapid and drivelling doggerel, sometimes scintillate indications of wit, humor, and positive genius.

Then there are theatrical "stars" and musical celebrities, with all their grandiloquent trumpet-blowing and tawdry belongings. In no profession or trade is advertising so much used and abused as in this. "Gorgeous scenery, new and costly dresses, decorations, and properties, with original and appropriate music *composed expressly* for this occasion!"—these rarely fail to go down with the public, although it is notorious that the first is a collection of vile daubs; the second, a parcel of worn-out trumpery; and the last a *potpourri* of hackneyed negro melodies and played-out street ditties. In this way slang is metamorphosed into wit; immodesty, into artistic grace; impudence, into talent; *la première danseuse,* into a divinity; the poor, underpaid *figurantes* and *coryphées,* into angels; and the whole tinsel-bedizened, flaring spectacle, into a veritable glimpse of fairyland. These are some of the consummations achieved by advertising.

Besides all this, there is a class of harpies who live more or less by their wits, and they find advertising often a profitable and remunerative game. "Astrological divinings," "medical quackery," "matrimonial openings," "business chances," offered to "energetic young men, *possessed of a little capital"* and "fortunes may be realized, and full particulars sent on receipt of twenty-five cents"—are a few of the creations of these human vultures, together with the execrable "Personals" which disfigure and disgrace the columns of our journals—for it is needless to say that all these, without exception, emanate from the same objectionable *coterie.* It appears almost incredible that these devices should succeed, or even pay for the expense of advertising; but that they *do* appear, is the best proof that they *do* pay; and this is in itself a very strong argument in support of the position we assumed at the outset, namely, that we are, all of us, occasionally liable to be taken in.

It is not only in America that this system obtains. In England and elsewhere it is quite as rife as on this side of the Atlantic. In fact, it was only the other day we were informed, on good authority, that Mr. Willan, a gentleman now at the head of two mammoth establishments in London and Paris, has amassed his colossal fortune within the last ten years, having, in that incredibly short space of time, risen to his present position of almost fabulous wealth from that of a common billposter, earning his daily wages with brush and pastepot! He now has the almost entire monopoly of that business in both the British and French metropolises, as well as on all the railroads and principal towns in both countries.

Advertising, from a mere convenience, has become a positive necessity, as well as a nuisance: stages, cars, steamboats, railroad depots, dead-walls, and boardings, are plastered over and actually papered with bills large and small, round and square, long and short; bills red, yellow, green, blue, and all the colors of the rainbow; nay, even the very rocks, stones, and stumps, are called into requisition, and, while these herald forth the praises of "Buchu" and the superior excellence of some cheap sensational periodical, we have a complete and literal realization of "tongues in trees . . . sermons in stones, and puffs in every thing!" It is, indeed, puff,

puff, puff, everywhere. We walk upon puffs, for the very sidewalks are stencilled with them; we rub shoulders with them, for there are living, peripatetic puff-mediums as well, with their clothes literally puffed with scarlet-and-gold letters; the air is full of them; they hang suspended across the roadway; they stream from the tops of lofty flagstaffs; they float from advertising balloons, and descend in fleecy showers from the roofs of advertising carriages; they are officiously crammed into our hand at every corner, into our pockets, or perchance even into our boots, if occasion offer; unfolding our morning paper, lo! a puff drops out of it, while the very piece of paper, which our obsequious barber lays on our shoulder to wipe his razor on, proves to be a puff of some abominable cosmetic, put there on purpose to stare us in the face and tempt us into reckless and unpardonable extravagance.

This system of advertising, we may observe, is a very ancient institution. It was known and in vogue more than two thousand years ago among the Romans, whose legal notices used to be "in public proposita," or "posted," in the Forum and other frequented places, with slave auctions advertised in terms very similar to the notices which, until lately, were common in the journals of our own Southern States. But advertising, as a system, was, in primitive times, a purely legitimate one; of that there can be little doubt, and its degeneracy nowadays can only be accounted for by the tremendous business competition at present existing. The jostle for supremacy is unceasing, and there are many people only too ready to resort to the most unworthy means to gain one rung on the ladder to wealth or preferment. It is such men as these that have diverted advertising from its fair and legitimate aim, and, by trying to vie with and outdo each other, have been the means of transmogrifying the old into a new system altogether, which, if it extends its ramifications in a ratio approximating in any way to its progress during the last ten years, bids fair to reduce trade to a mere scramble, and the majority of our merchants and storekeepers to the grade of shifty charlatans and blatant "Cheap Johns."

Chapter 12

Noise and Health

John H. Girdner, M. D.

There is no question but that the confusing and discordant noises of large cities are detrimental to the health of those who are obliged to dwell in them for the greater part of the year. The injury to health from this source is not entirely of a local character. In fact, the irritation to the auditory apparatus—that is, the ear itself, its nerves, and its other appendages—is of less importance than the harm done to the brain and general nervous system by the roar and din of modern cities.

We are often disposed to forget the very important part which the five senses play in the physical life of the individual. It is only by means of his powers of hearing, seeing, smelling, tasting, and feeling that man is able to come in contact at all with the material universe around him. Imagine the condition of a person totally blind and deaf, and with entire loss of the senses of smell, taste, and touch. He would be reduced almost to the condition of a tree. His heart might continue to beat, breathing would go on, digestion

Reprinted from John H. Girdner, M.D., "Noise and Health," in *Munsey's Magazine,* 25 (June, 1901), 323–326.

and assimilation of food need not be interfered with, and mere animal existence could continue indefinitely; but he would be absolutely isolated. He could gain no information of the world around him, nor could he communicate in any way whatsoever with his fellowmen.

All our information with regard to objects of nature, and all communications from our fellows, must pass through one or more of these channels, consequently the five senses are the means of all conscious relation with the external world.

Noise and the Nerves

This intimate and important relation between the brain and general nervous system, on the one hand, and each of the nerves of special sense, makes it apparent that impressions made upon any one of the five senses must have a more or less powerful influence upon the brain and nerves of the entire body. Now, if the impressions made upon the five senses, on any one of them, are pronounced and painful, and of constant recurrence—as, for instance, when a bright light is constantly flashed before the eyes, or loud and discordant noises are poured in on the nerves of the ear—they cannot fail to produce irritation and exhaustion of the brain and nerves all over the body; and in this way the general health is made to suffer.

The roar and din of a modern city causes almost constant irritation to the nervous system through the auditory apparatus, and this irritation in turn results in a lowering of the general health and resisting power of the individual. Noise thus plays an important part in producing neurasthenia, or nervous prostration, a disease of cities and of modern civilization. Aside from the destructive effect on the general health, noise produces local changes in the ear itself which sometimes amount to chronic inflammation, and very often to partial deafness.

There is a disease known as "boiler makers' deafness." It was discovered and described many years ago, when a boiler factory was the noisiest of places. A considerable percentage of men who had worked at the trade for a long time were found to be more or less deaf, hence the names of the disease. It is caused by the violent concussions to which the delicate structures of the internal ear are constantly subjected by the infernal din of hammering upon the resonant iron. When the eardrum and other structures are constantly compelled to withstand these concussions, and the frequently repeated mechanical violence of loud and discordant noises, they become much thicker and tougher than is natural, and are unable to respond to the more delicate vibrations of the sounds produced in ordinary conversation.

The boiler factory no longer has a monopoly in producing this affection. The streets of our modern cities are becoming so noisy that unless the evil is abated by improved pavements and means of traffic, the name of the disease will have to be changed to the "city dweller's deafness."

The Noise Habit

The New Yorker in time contracts what may be called the noise habit. Noise with him becomes a dissipation. His nervous system demands it. This is illustrated by the sensations he experiences when he goes into the woods or mountains after a continuous stay in the city for many months. His first feeling is one of loneliness; something seems to have suddenly gone out of his life. Every tree seems to say, "Why have you been so hot and noisy, my little sir?" His sensations are somewhat akin to those of a drunkard who has been under alcoholic stimulation for a long time, and suddenly has his drink taken from him. His whole nervous system feels the lack of the irritation and stimulation of the city noise, to which it has become accustomed. The stillness actually appals and depresses him.

The noise habit, like every other, grows by what it feeds upon, and this artificial stimulant has gained such a hold that the New Yorker requires it with his dinner. Just as his stomach demands the stimulating effect of a cocktail before the meal, so his nervous system demands noise during it, and in these latter years no hotel or restaurant can hope for patronage which does not furnish a noisy band of music with the food it sells. If there is one time more than every other when the brain and nervous system should be free from thought and excitation of every kind, it is during the dinner hour. The blood is required in the stomach to furnish a plentiful flow of gastric secretion; yet our modern cafés are a pandemonium of loud talking, music, and general racket. The effect of such surroundings on the mind and emotions cannot fail to be detrimental to the digestion and assimilation of food. The stomach that requires a cocktail to arouse the appetite, and the nervous system that demands the stimulating effect of an orchestra in order to enjoy a dinner, are both in an abnormal, unnatural, and unhealthy condition.

There has been a steady increase of noise in the streets of New York during the last ten years. Asphalt pavements and rubber tires promised welcome relief; they are more than offset by the clanging electric and cable cars and whirring automobiles. The elevated road is like the poor; we have it with us always. Another cause of the great increase of the din and roar in the streets is the modern skyscraper. Its high walls furnish a greatly increased surface for the reverberation of sound waves, and the noise is thus intensified many times.

The streets of New York are deep, narrow channels, and they are growing constantly deeper, as the buildings increase in height. These large reflecting surfaces on three sides of him make the condition of the man in the street like that of the workman who suffers from reflected noise while he hammers rivets on the inside of a boiler.

The Contrast of City and Country

It has been pointed out how continual exposure to harsh and discordant noises will produce local trouble in previously healthy ears; and also what an important factor this is in neurasthenia, or nervous prostration. If those who were previously well can be so seriously affected in this way, it is plain that invalids and persons suffering from diseases of all kinds, both acute and chronic, must have recovery retarded when they are obliged to remain in the babel of noises which surrounds them in most parts of the city. In selecting sites for hospitals, and in contructing them, one of the most important considerations is to shut out, so far as possible, all noise from the streets, and to secure, as nearly as may be, perfect silence in the wards and rooms. Every one knows how important rest and quiet are for the recovery of the sick; yet every physician who practises in a large city must know how hard it is to secure such a condition. In many instances it is a luxury which money cannot buy. When we send patients from the city to the country, it is not alone the change of air and scene which is desirable, but also the rural peace and quiet, and freedom from the city's constant shock and concussion to the brain and nervous system.

One often hears expressed a general belief that people who live for a long time in the city get used to the noise and do not mind it. This is true in a sense, just as it is true that the drunkard gets used to alcohol, and that the opium fiend can take larges doses of his favorite drug. The New Yorker goes about his business apparently unconscious of the thousands of ear splitting and brain bruising noises pouring into his auditory canals every instant. By long practice, he has become an expert in paying no attention to sounds which do not concern him for the moment. But his ability to entertain in his sensorium only such sounds as interest him does not prevent other noises from proving unconscious irritants to his nerves.

This point is well illustrated when the man from the rural district visits a large city for the first time. He appears at a great disadvantage; not because his thinking machinery is not as good as that of those who laugh at him, for it is often better. The country man's trouble is that he sees and hears too many things, or, rather, he allows his sensorium to entertain all the sights and sounds brought to it by his eyes and ears, with the result that he is overpowered and confused, and presents a ludicrous spectacle. He has not learned the city man's art of entertaining only such sounds as he chooses. The country man is exhausted after a day in the city. His nervous system is no more fit to withstand this extra and unaccustomed strain and irritation than is the city man's muscular system capable of performing a day's labor on the farm.

The Need of Legislation

In the century just closing, Christian civilization has done more to protect health, cure disease, and increase man's physical comfort, than has been accomplished during any similar period in the world's history. New scientific discoveries relating to the cause and prevention of diseases and the cure of injuries, and practical inventions catering to our physical comfort, have followed one another in rapid succession, especially in the last twenty-five years. All these, supplemented by wise legislation, have greatly reduced the death rate and the sick list throughout the civilized world. Lawmakers and experimenters are steadily engaged on plans to improve the health and comfort of mankind. It is a little curious, in view of these facts, that practically nothing has been done to lessen the powerful and nerve-racking noises which fill the streets of civilized cities and towns. The other senses have been protected by legislation, but the sense of hearing has been left to its fate, and any one is at liberty to assault the nervous system through this channel without molestation.

Effective municipal warfare has been made against smoke and offensive odors, which are disagreeable, but which do not constitute any material menace to health. Noise is not only equally disagreeable, but is positively health destroying; yet there are practically no city ordinances against it. One small success has been won by the foes of noise—just enough to show that further reform is possible. In 1896 the New York board of aldermen were induced to pass an ordinance making it a misdemeanor punishable by a fine of twenty-five dollars to haul wagons loaded with iron beams through the streets, unless the free ends were wrapped so as to prevent them from knocking against each other. A few drivers were arrested and fined for violating this ordinance, and as a result we are rid of one of the worst and most brain bruising noises from which New Yorkers suffered.

Of course, the business of a great city cannot be carried on without noise, and a great deal of noise; but a little study and observation will show that fully half of the ear-splitting racket of the streets is unnecessary, and could be prevented by well-considered legislation without any injury to business and without the slightest interference with individual rights.

Six Kinds of City Noises

City noises may be classified under the six following heads:
  1. Noises produced by wheeled vehicles of any kind, and by the animals—usually horses, or sometimes mules—drawing them.

2. Noises produced by street peddlers, hucksters, hawkers, musicians, and so forth.

3. Noises produced by bells, whistles, horns, clocks, etc.

4. Noises produced by animals, other than those drawing vehicles—as cats, dogs, or birds.

5. Explosives.

6. All noises which come from the inside of our houses, as persons learning to play musical instruments or training the voice, and the loud talking and screeching that one often hears at fashionable functions.

We will select a few examples of noise from each of the above classes, and, where possible, point out how they might be abolished or at least abated. When all the New York streets were paved with stone blocks, the passage of a carriage and horses was very disturbing, but asphalt pavements and rubber tires have done away with the noise, except the clatter of the horses' feet. Underground rapid transit ought sooner or later to reduce the number of clanging cable cars and roaring elevated trains.

Nearly all the street noises in group two are unnecessary. A city ordinance making it a misdemeanor for any person to shout his wares in the streets, and compelling the rag and bottle men and scissors grinders to ring the basement bell and inquire if their services are wanted would rid the streets in the residence quarters of intolerable nuisances. Such an ordinance would in no way injure the business of these people; it would in some respects prove an advantage to them. The sale of newspapers by strong lunged men yelling "Extra!" in the streets is a direct infringement on the rights of the residents. I can produce cases where the lives of sick persons were shortened by the continual shouting of "Extra!" under their windows during the war with Spain.

One of the worst and seemingly most useless noise makers in our third group is the church bell. It is hard to see any practical reason for its existence. When congregations were scattered, and when watches were a rare luxury, bells were of service to notify the people of the hour of worship. Today they are useless disturbers of the Sunday morning quiet, which is so refreshing to many, tired out with the week's toil.

In the fourth class we find cats. I know of no reason why cats should be permitted to infest streets and back yards and destroy sleep by their nightly vocal exercises. Children are quite as likely to be bitten and scratched by them as by dogs, yet under existing regulations stray dogs are promptly taken to the pound and destroyed, while the cats are allowed to remain.

Explosives compose the fifth class. We should be thankful that this torture is mostly confined to one day in the year, the Fourth of July. An ordinance against the use of explosives in the city streets should be passed and enforced, and if young America must express his patriotism in barbarous noises, make him go into the country to do it.

Of the sixth group—noises from the inside of our houses—we have little to say. If people are so unthinking and ill-bred as to have no consideration for their neighbors in the matter of noise in their own dwellings, nothing I can say will have any effect. Persistent disturbances of this sort may, of course, be suppressed by lodging a complaint with the municipal health board.

Chapter 13

The Pressure of Population

William S. Rossiter

Immense increase in the world's population was the most important legacy from the nineteenth century to the twentieth. No achievements in the field of science during that period will exercise such far-reaching influence on future generations as the unparalleled increase which occurred in the number of human beings.

This decided change in world population has assumed a significance hitherto unknown. Widely extended decrease in the number of human beings would tend ultimately to disorganize the economic structure of society; on the other hand, over liberal increase for a considerable period, or inflation of population, would create new and grave problems, perhaps resulting in even greater demoralization than would be caused by decrease.

In earlier ages insecurity of life and property, especially the prevalence of war, famine, and pestilence, frequently transferred entire tribes or nations for long periods into the nonproductive

Reprinted from William S. Rossiter, "The Pressure of Population," in *Atlantic Monthly,* 108 (December, 1911), 836-843.

class; but in our time increasing civilization and stability of government have created for each human being a distinct economic value, and in consequence every man and woman possesses a minute but definite place in the vast mosaic of human activities.

Already the race has responded to this stimulation to an extraordinary degree. It becomes important, therefore, to consider whether rapid increase in world population is likely to continue indefinitely, and whether new problems, which may be termed population phenomena, are beginning to manifest themselves because of the noteworthy increase which already has occurred.

During most of the long period for which there is historical record the number of human beings on the earth doubtless was comparatively small. More than a century ago, in his essay upon "The Populousness of Ancient Nations," David Hume brought together, with singular patience and learning, the scanty comments of Greek and Roman writers concerning the number of inhabitants in ancient cities and states. According to Hume, the aggregate population must have been insignificant, when judged by modern standards.

The total population of Greece, except Laconia, in the period of Philip of Macedon, approximated 1,300,000. Ancient Athens, at the time of her great prosperity, probably contained less then 300,000 inhabitants, according to Hume's estimate, based on Xenophon's computation of 10,000 houses. The number of houses in Rome, in her glory, was probably between forty and fifty thousand; so the population of the Mistress of the World may have approximated 1,500,000 in her prime, but even this figure is probably overliberal. These estimates, it must be remembered, include great numbers of slaves.

Continual warfare, famines, plagues, private strifes, and political massacres, aided by universal slavery which withdrew large numbers of potential parents of both sexes from the reproducing class, undoubtedly held down the population of the world in ancient times to a small total. Moreover, under the control of these "parasites," the aggregate of the earth's inhabitants seems to have fluctuated from century to century within rather narrow limits. Signor Bodio, the accomplished Director of the Italian Census Bureau, estimates that at the death of Augustus, the entire world contained not more than 54,000,000 human beings. If this estimate be accepted, an increase of a little more than twenty percent per century would produce our present world population, and a considerably smaller percentage of increase per century would have produced the total population actually living on the earth in 1800. There seems, however, to have been no appreciable change in ability, desire, or willingness to reproduce, although before the nineteenth century human life and the home in all nations were frequently, and often for long periods, extremely insecure. Mortality from numerous causes was so great that the birth rate must have been high, merely to have maintained numbers without increase.

The tendency toward stationary population manifested through the ages makes it not unreasonable to suppose that if political, economic, and industrial conditions had continued practically the same throughout the nineteenth century as at the period when Malthus declared that population was limited by means of subsistence, changes during the century would have varied little from those which occurred during previous centuries.

The extraordinary quickening of industrial acitvty which in the nineteenth century attended the application of steam to manufacture and transportation, the progress of the world in scientific knowledge, and in liberal and enlightened government, and the decrease of warfare, created entirely new conditions, all of which tended to stimulate increase in the number of human beings. India practically doubled in population, reaching in 1900 the huge total of 290,000,000. The population of Europe and the number of persons of European stock increased from about 125,000,000 in 1750 to 500,000,000 in 1900. Moreover, the European exercised a stimulating effect upon other races with which he came in contact. In short, the human race increased about fity percent in numbers, or from approximately a billion in 1800 to a billion-and-a-half in 1900. The remarkable increase in the number of human beings during the last century, or a little more, is thus clearly at variance with the previous experience of the race.

It is significant that the increase here noted tended, especially in more civilized nations, to create large numbers of cities of great size. In 1900 there were two hundred cities in the world with a population exceeding 100,000 but less than 250,000, eighty-four with from 250,000 to 1,000,000, and seventeen which exceeded 1,000,000. These three hundred cities aggregated 100,000,000 population. Here again is a phenomenon of population, new in our time.

In France, in one hundred years a group of specified cities increased four-fold, while the nation, exclusive of these municipalities, increased little more than twenty percent. Stated in another way, the urban population increased 6,500,000, and the remainder of France but 5,100,000. The population of large cities, which in 1801 was less than one-tenth of all, had become a century later one-quarter of all the French people. In England, rather insufficient data indicate that the cities increased over six-fold, and the remainder of England and Wales about two-and-one-half-fold. The urban population, one-quarter of all in 1801, a century later constituted more than one-half of all.

In the United States, the urban increase approximated one hundred-fold. That of the remainder of the population about eleven-fold. Economic conditions in this age of industrial activity, and the urban tendency resulting from it, are sharply at variance with those which prevailed in antiquity. "I do not remember a passage in any early author," declares Dr. Hume, "where the growth of a city is ascribed to the establishment of a manufacture. The commerce which is said to flourish is chiefly the exchange of those commodities for which different soils and climates are suited."

Thus far, attention has been especially invited to these facts:

1. The population of the world prior to 1800 was comparatively small.

2. The increase from age to age was exceedingly slow, and the general tendency of humanity to maintain rather small numbers showed no striking change.

3. During the century from 1800 to 1900 the hindrances to the increase of human beings, in general the same as those established by nature to limit the increase of other living creatures, were largely overcome by civilized man; and in addition, entirely new industrial conditions developed, which offered means of support for many millions of people.

4. In consequence, the number of human beings on the globe increased to an extraordinary degree, and at the close of the nineteenth century, the population of the world exceeded a billion-and-a-half.

5. Principally under the influence of industrial activity, mankind has tended more and more to concentrate in large cities.

These facts create the impression that nature tended to limit men to reasonable numbers, and to pass the globe on from the possession of one generation to that of the next with little depreciation. Viewing the earth as a vast property, one may claim that the tribes of men have been mere tenants upon it from age to age. They cultivated small areas of the richer portions, scratched the surface for minerals, and utilized beasts of burden and windpower for purposes of commerce and transportation. In consequence, "the tenants" bequeathed the property to their posterity in good condition.

Until the nineteenth century, the vast stored up wealth of the earth had been practically unimpaired through all recorded history. Within the last hundred years, however, the influences by which an equilibrium of population had been previously maintained appear to have been overcome by mankind, and nature has been forced to stop paying an annuity, and to some extent to yield up the principal. The present age, in consequence, witnesses unprecedented numbers of human beings, and a feverish attack all over the world upon the earth's resources of forest, field, and mine.

The significance of this fact is best appreciated by imagining the population of the earth at the beginning of the Christian era to have been the same as it was in 1900, and that it began an attack upon natural resources in the first century with the vigor with which it is conducted in the twentieth. Assuming such attack to have continued and increased for nineteen hundred years, it takes little reflection to reach a state of gratitude to nature that she succeeded so long in holding mankind down in numbers and in supporting them upon an "annuity."

But if a variety of causes have contributed to invite very large human increase in a comparatively brief period, does it also follow that these influences will never spend themselves, and that a liberal increase of world population will continue indefinitely? An affirmative answer to this question does not appear to be reasonable. If, for example, the increase of world population should continue at the nineteenth-century rate, five hundred years later, in 2400, the world would be supporting thirteen-and-one-half billions of human beings.

Obviously, somewhere there must be bounds, though perhaps distant ones, to the multiplication of humanity. If so, what are the methods by which nature will again effect the limitation of numbers? Since man has overcome and passed beyond the cruder means of retarding increase, as war, pestilence, and famine, what natural law will be encountered, or become increasingly effective, to produce the same result?

It must be remembered that as increase of population progresses, the mere fact of increase creates new conditions. These in turn may check or destroy earlier tendencies. Thus, out of the great increase in population in our time, has come already at least one significant fact. This may be termed "the pressure of population." It is the general instinctive realization of large numbers. Expression of this realization appears in the decreasing belief that personal responsibility rests on the individual to rear a large family, or even, in many cases, to become a parent. Mere numbers— the pressure of humanity on all sides, expecially in the large cities —constitute ever-present evidence to the average man and woman that there are people enough, and the struggle for existence is too severe already to be increased by unnecessary burdens. In consequence, there has arisen a rather remarkable and widespread tendency, now clearly evident in most of the larger communities of Europe, voluntarily to limit the family. The effect of this tendency is most marked in France, where it has produced a present state of equilibrium of population liable to be changed at any time into a positive national decrease. Limitation of family has also appeared in other parts of the world and has caused much concern in Australia, where a very small total white population is shown. It should not be overlooked, however, in connection with the apparently exceptional problem presented by Australia, that the southern Continent seems never to have sustained a large population. The aborigines of Australia, New Zealand, and Tasmania were not numerous, and those that remain are dying out so rapidly as to suggest a very frail racial grasp upon existence.

In the United States, the conditions have tended more and more to approximate those of Europe. From the pioneer stage which prevailed when Malthus called attention to the phenomenal fertility of many American communities, the nation has advanced so far and with such rapidity that the change constitutes one of the marvels of the age. By a sort of forced draught, secured with the assistance of all Europe, the United States has attained an eighteen-fold increase in population in one hundred years. The national policy during this era of feverish development may be summed up as a continuous and successful attempt to compress the normal national growth of a long period into a few decades.

Beginning as an agricultural nation, the American people have been turning more and more toward mining and industrial operations upon a vast scale. Both citizens of native stock and newly arrived immigrants have drifted to manufacturing and commercial centers, until nearly one-third of the inhabitants of the United States now live in cities containing more than 20,000 inhabitants. This, it must be remembered, has occurred in a nation possessing vast areas of rich land, much of which is not cultivated. In consequence of this national tendency, already there are large sections of the United States in which the pressure of population has become clearly evident. But one other city in the world now exceeds New York in population, and doubtless at no distant period the American city will be the largest on the earth in numbers. Within her limits are nearly 5,000,000 human beings. The actual pressure of population in such a vast aggregation of races, temperaments, ambitions, and purposes, representing all degrees of success and failure, of hope and hopelessness, of good and evil, can only be likened to the pressure of the ocean at great depths.

In consequence, it is not strange that in the United States also has appeared the modern tendency to limit the family. It has become so general, indeed, in many sections, that the effect upon the states and the nation in all probability would be more evident even than it is in France, if it were not concealed by immigration. Substantially all the national increase is now contributed by the later stock, and by persons born in other countries and their children.

The conditions and practice here alluded to have been aggressively and very justly assailed as being destructive to domestic happiness, character building, and national stability. To these assertions there can be no effective reply.

The large family has been, and is, one of the principal sources of the finer elements of American character. The United States is what it is today because of large families. Their decrease should be a cause of much concern. It is useless, however, to ignore world tendencies. If, in response to a conscientious conviction that larger families were proper and necessary for the welfare of the nation, the American people should increase the proportion of children to that which prevailed in 1790, there would be added nearly 16,000,000 to the total population. The continuation of this rate of increase added to the present actual increase (derived largely from external sources) would advance the population of the United States by leaps and bounds. Without radical change in the wants and consumption of each individual, in other words, without an economic revolution, such increase obviously could not long continue.

The American people, almost instinctively, have turned away from the old domestic policy. A large family implies a home in the old-fashioned sense, but the urban life of America necessitates a departure from the home as thus defined. The cramped apartment, with those ministering angels, the kitchenette, the baker, the laundryman and delicatessen shop, are not adapted to numerous children. Children often are not wanted. In fact, a man with a large family finds it difficult in many cities even to secure living accommodations. Thus, in great numbers of communities, the social order has passed beyond the conviction that the large family is a normal and necessary condition, and has adapted itself to a scale of living based on small families, or none at all.

The significance of this new phase of human fertility, or lack of it, clearly lies in the fact that it is worldwide. A practice which is almost as common among the Negroes of the Mississippi "black belt" as in Paris or New York, cannot be summarily dismissed as a crime or as a sign of degeneracy. If the age-old natural methods of checking increase, such as war, pestilence, and famine, which may be termed the external methods, have been eliminated, clearly other means of limitation, if any there are to be, must arise from within, from voluntary action, responsive to instinct. This at once suggests the question whether nature is not utilizing for purposes of limitation the pressure of population, now so evident in many parts of the world, as a modern substitute for the agencies effective in earlier periods, but now ineffective. In short, is not the increasing inclination shown by a vast multitude of civilized humanity to check excessive increase of population obedience to a new instinctive impulse? Obviously the inquirer is compelled to look far beyond such evident local causes of limitation as wealth, selfishness, and fashion, often ascribed as the actual causes.

But if, as thus suggested, the race is now becoming obedient to new population influences, whither do they lead us? In the past, the crude limitations of population incidentally tended to strengthen the character and increase the endeavor of those who survived. In this age, by wonderful invention and achievement, we have directly stimulated increase in numbers; but if in so doing we have brought into operation new forces or influences which in turn war insidiously against further pronounced increase, we may have entailed much ultimate injury upon society by affecting one of the main sources of human strength and progress. When individuals of both sexes, oppressed by the pressure of population on all sides and convinced that the race is increasing without their aid, or that it already is too numerous without increase, feel themselves absolved from the performance of the supreme natural function, society is confronted with a problem of the gravest importance. The avoidance of having children has become already so general that the man of intelligence and influence who rears a large family is now both exceptional and courageous. Thus the age-old instinct, for the quickening of which farsighted statesmen in this and other countries are pleading, seems to have been dulled. The energy which, under the old conditions, would be devoted to the rearing of children is now largely turned in other directions. It seldom benefits the state and society, but is generally expended upon some form, however innocent, of self-gratification.

No defense is here implied of blind and unreasoning increase in communities or nations which cannot offer their offspring opportunity for support. Such increase, of which China presents an illustration, becomes a source of weakness. This fact, however, rather heightens the significance of the opposite policy of deliberate limitation exemplified in France, where it has resulted in loss of political prestige, and has not eased the strain upon social and economic life. In the United States the pressure of population is manifested in the steadily decreasing fertility of the older and what are called the better, and certainly the more stable, elements of society.

Innumerable races and tribes have died out as the centuries have passed, and there are nations and races dying out in various parts of the globe at the present time. In general, this results, in the case of human beings as in that of animals, from uncongenial environment. Instinct probably dictates to each sex a reluctance to produce offspring which shall be subjected to conditions deemed unsatisfactory. This fact suggests the sinister possibilities which lurk in the shadow of the new influences upon population —since equilibrium or slight increase borders close upon decrease.

France is an illustration of the futility of attempting to control natural functions by mere public appeal.

If the large family is the most wholesome state for society, then its decline must be a distinct loss. Moreover, this loss comes at a period of time when more better men are needed than in any previous period. Never before has the race been called upon to administer and increase such a vast accumulation of knowledge, or to deal with such a complexity in the social order.

These considerations suggest that perhaps the human race, in its magnificent endeavor in this age, has in reality overreached itself and sown the seeds of decay. It is possible to imagine stationary and then decreasing population as becoming at length worldwide, and finally a distinct downward movement of the race, as though humanity were burnt out by over-excitement, wealth, and excess. Mankind is no longer young; is the race to be always virile?

Science and civilization waged successful war upon the population parasites of the past by removing them. It is unlikely that in the future the new form of limitation can be so completely disposed of. But it is reasonable to expect that the nations, perceiving that the limitation of progeny—with its attendant drawbacks—has become a definite instinctive tendency, will attempt the supremely difficult task of securing a higher average of men and women, by preventing reproduction by criminals and incompetents, and by increasing scientific breeding. If the state is confronted by limited reproduction, it cannot afford to allow the weak, incompetent, insane and feebleminded to thrust their tainted progeny upon the community, as now occurs to a serious degree. The race must be perpetuated by those most competent to produce the best men and women.

There will be also another cause for future concern. In the past, by a rather cruel process, breeding was generally accomplished by the physically fit, since those who were not fit died of disease or were killed off. A marked change, however, has now occurred. All the discoveries and resources of modern medicine, surgery, and sanitation are exerted, not only to prolong the lives of the physically unfit and to set them upon their feet, but also to enable them to contribute an appreciable proportion to the next generation. In earlier periods most of the graduates of modern hospitals would have died off without leaving issue; doubtless the race was much better off physically.

Summed up, the history of the world in all earlier ages is a record of the substitution of a virile and fertile tribe for one inferior in these essentials. Here also the past is likely to offer no precedent for the future. Modern progress has revolutionized so many of the conditions of life that migration of races and extensive conquest grow less and less possible. The tragic substitution of strong nations for weaker ones is likely to be superseded by slow internal changes affecting many nations.

Have we no sign or intimation of what these changes will be?

Here, perhaps, we of this generation should pause. Solution of these sobering problems assuredly lies not with us, but with those who shall follow long after us. This period of ours has overturned all precedent by creating human beings in numbers far in excess of those in any previous age, and has revolutionized industrial and economic conditions; but in this great adventure, we have embarked on a voyage upon an uncharted sea.

> Twelve hundred million men are spread
> About this earth, and I and You
> Wonder, when You and I are dead,
> What will these luckless millions do?

Chapter 14

American Wastefulness

Austin Bierbower

Nowhere in the world is there such a waste of material as in this country. In our eagerness to get the most results from our resources, and to get them quickly, we destroy perhaps as much as we use. Americans have not learned to save; and their wastefulness imperils their future. Our resources are fast giving out, and the next problem will be to make them last.

In passing the alleys of an American city, a foreigner marvels at the quantity of produce in the garbage boxes. The thrifty Germans would have saved this; and there is no excuse for letting it spoil in these days of cold storage and quick transportation.

Our families are proverbially wasteful in their homes. It is said that two Frenchmen can live off what one American wastes and live better than the American. We do not utilize things closely, as others do, but serve only our best provisions when all might be used. We do not, for example, save apple parings, which a German housewife boils to get bits of pulp for soup or sauce. At the table,

Reprinted from Austin Bierbower, "American Wastefulness," in *Overland Monthly,* 49 (April, 1907), 358–359.

Americans often leave as much on their plates as is eaten, whereas abroad, it is thought vulgar to leave anything on the plate. And since foreigners eat everything given them, no more than enough is served.

Until recently there was a criminal waste at our slaughter houses. Only the best portions of meat were saved for market. Now all is used, and the by-products made from what was once the offal, are often enough to pay the expenses of the business. We are beginning to make the most of our resources, as foreigners do, and we must get into the habit of doing this with all our materials if we are to compete successfully with foreigners in supplying the markets.

A German or Frenchman going by where one of our buildings is being demolished, is struck with the fires that are built to burn up the materials. Much good timber goes up in smoke, besides firewood, which in Europe would be gathered up and sold for kindling. When decayed cedar blocks are taken from the pavements, we find it hard to get anybody to carry them away. Abroad the poor would gladly use them. We think here that the time required to haul them away is worth more than their value as fuel.

If one should follow a coal wagon through one of our cities, he might pick up enough coal to warm him through the winter. In Europe every small piece is saved. It would not be allowed, in the first place, to fall from the wagon; and if it should fall, there would be a dozen to pick it up. Enough oats and corn is scattered in the streets of one of our cities to feed all the poultry raised within its limits. People think it cheaper to haul big loads than to save what falls off. This extravagance comes to us, as to most pioneers in civilization, because labor is scarcer than materials. When our country was first settled, the problem of the people was to get quick results from their toil. They cultivated only the best land and raised the greatest crops. Much of the time of our fathers was spent in cutting away forests. In Indiana, until recently, the people cut down oak and walnut trees which would now be worth a hundred dollars each, and rolled them into heaps to be burned. A statistician has figured out the loss sustained by this wastefulness, and he claims that if all the lumber which was destroyed to make farms were now in our possession, it would be worth more than all the agricultural products that have been raised on those lands since the settlement of our country. A like waste is still seen in Oregon,

Washington, and Alaska. The forests are destroyed along with the trees, and only a little of the tree is used.

There was at first a like waste of coal. Only the solid parts were used; the vast quantities of culm and dust, which are now so valuable, were thrown away. Half of our coal was thus lost in the mining, and people are now trying to recover it from the beds of rivers and banks of refuse. As our coal is giving out in many places, and an end of it is in sight for the whole country, the saving is becoming a greater problem than the mining.

The sawdust and bark of trees were formerly wasted. Now we have important uses for them; but so little remains that it cannot be made available, as when it was produced in enormous quantities. With the burning of the refuse of the mills, and the destruction by fire of forests, we are poorer by hundreds of millions than if we had cared for these resources, as foreigners do.

Our farmers early got into a wastefulness that is now continued even after their land has become valuable. We do not cultivate all that might be cultivated. Millions of acres are allowed to lie fallow, which would yield boundless riches; but the people do not care to till any but the best. An American farmer wastes as much in fence corners as a foreigner could live on. In Germany there are rarely any fences at all, but narrow swards of grass serve for boundaries, or a few stakes along which the eye traces a beeline. While great fields are used in America to pasture a few calves, the calves are elsewhere chained to a spot only large enough to support them.

In building there is a like waste. Temporary structures are erected to be taken down in a few years; dwelling houses that cost thousands of dollars are removed to put up shops, which are expected soon to give way again to permanent buildings. It is not uncommon in Chicago to take down a six story structure to erect a higher one. Nowhere else is there such a waste of buildings. People seem incapable of looking far ahead when they first build, and so do not build permanently.

Alterations of great expense are yearly made for tenants, which do not improve the property. Our people quickly adjust themselves to what they want; which is wasteful if they know not what that is. Many of the alterations made are soon changed back again, and there is a successive series of wastes. For trifling conveniences, great expenses are incurred, and our buildings are more altered than those in the larger cities of any other country.

Nowhere is there so much money spent as in America in open-ing new streets and widening old ones. As great incompetence marks the laying out of cities, equal incompetence is afterwards shown in changing the plan. Miles of business houses are some-times torn down for slight advantages, which are often but tempo-rary. It is proposed in Chicago to widen Halsted street for four miles, at a cost of fifteen millions, when there are parallel streets near it on both sides which suffice for the traffic. London for centu-ries had no parallel street within half a mile of the Strand, its greatest thoroughfare, and yet the people never thought, until recently, of opening a new street, or even of widening that one. Streets are here opened through parks, because the people do not want to go a few yards around, so that often more damage than benefit results from the changes made.

In general, we have not learned to utilize our resources. We have had so much that it has been harder to save then to accumu-late. But now, with the coming of a poor class, it becomes a ques-tion of saving, if only to give the surplus to the needy. We cannot safely continue our extravagance as the country becomes crowded, and there is only enough produced to support the popu-lation. When one wastes, many suffer, and the suffering cannot go much farther without endangering those who have an abundance.

Part V

New Law and Order

New Law and Order

Police work, like fire fighting, underwent a technological revolution. Street lighting, call boxes, improved transportation, and better firearms affected police routine. Inside precinct houses, a growing body of experts worked with fingerprints, photographs, dossiers, and laboratory equipment. A new class of detectives could cooperate quickly with other police agencies via the telephone or telegraph.

As in other sectors of life, these changes promoted dispatch, efficiency, and predictability. They also sharpened the policeman's consciousness of himself. But society was quicker to give law enforcement agents more equipment than to improve their status or redefine their roles. The average policeman worked for low wages, in poor circumstances, and was not trained to deal with new social problems like drug abuse or juvenile warfare. Municipal reformers and experts attacked the corruption that so often flourished in police work, and tried to improve both the police officer's condition and preparation.

The same reform elements tried to revamp the prison system. Prisoners had no political leverage to exact attention, but reformers and penologists worked to turn the prison ideal from incarceration to rehabilitation. They also sought to humanize the penal process, and crusaded against the death penalty. Public indifference, costs, and the jumble of state-local-federal jurisdictions hampered any systematic prison reform. But the new type of administrator had some impact in prison work, especially in the federal system.

The poverty behind some crime also received closer scrutiny. Workers in tenement reform advertised the need for better housing, health and sanitation services. But a general notion that anyone with talent could attain affluence kept the reality of poverty at the edge of public consciousness. Yet some analysts began to see the full effects of poverty, the myths that hampered remedial action, and the state of the poor.

Chapter 15

The Police Problem

William Ralston Balch

The most conspicuous failure of American civilization is the American policeman. He is the bar sinister on the shield of every American city; an amazing satire on our love and reverence for the law. Were he merely a failure as an element of our social structure it would not be so bad, but he is everywhere the supreme disgrace of the day, a disgrace that yearly grows more and more patent, and more and more offensive. Corruption flourishes in the policeman's care, crime waxes fierce and careless, and a large premium is placed on brutality—masquerading as authority —of which he is the foremost type.

Being that visible form of the law most familiar to the people, he should have instilled respect, fear, and obedience. He has succeeded everywhere in exciting contempt, disrespect, and revolt. To make fun of the police, to sneer at their efficiency, to laugh at their clumsy attempts at detection, have grown to be, through police incompetence, instincts of all city dwellers. The policeman

Reprinted from William Ralston Balch, "The Police Problem," in *International Review,* 13 (December, 1882), 507–517.

is invariably made ridiculous on the stage, he is unanimously lam-
pooned in the papers, he is universally "sassed" in the streets, on
duty or off; but preferably while on duty, for then he is the puny,
limping majesty of the law.

One of the wizened officers who kept the sacred peace of Salem
city, a tall, aged man, borrowed possibly from a Hawthorne romance or left behind by some careless century, remarked on one
occasion that "more people were arrested for sassing the police
than for any other crime." Shades of Claude Duval! Yet this, to a
serious degree, is the modern policeman's idea of how the law
should be upheld. He demands instant obedience to anything he
may say, and if he does not get it repeats the sentence in choice
profanity, often punctuating his words with his club, or he drags
the innocent remonstrant to the lockup on a charge of "disorderly
conduct." Disobedience to himself is held to be a greater offense
than disobedience to the law. With this idea of the statutes he
terrifies small boys and women—the criminal classes never. They
know that he is slow, sleepy-eyed, and corrupt. "Two policemen,"
says a floating paragraph, "met last night on opposite corners of
Broadway at Grand street. Says the first comer, 'Moike, are yez
there?' Answers the second comer, 'Well, yer can bate yer shwate
loife I'm there or thereabouts.' " How thoroughly this is appreciated by the criminal! How essentially our policeman is "thereabouts" and not "there!" How universal it is to find him
represented in the hour of necessity by X, an unknown quantity!

As a man the nowadays policeman is brutal, ignorant, stupid; or
brutal, fairly educated, cunning. From the second is manufactured
an officer; the first always remains a private. Officer or private, his
instincts have never had the training that controls nor the cultivation that refines. The appointing power asks of him, Who wants
you appointed? How tall are you? How strong? If the answer to the
first question is satisfactory a uniform is then brought, and so
wonderful is its make that an ignorant blackguard, when thrust
into it, becomes at once a capable officer, whose intelligence, virtue, courage, and sobriety are vouched for with the star of authority. Yet this same officer, when on duty, is more apt to be drunk
than sober; he knows no law other than his own passion; he uses
profane and vulgar language, to the shame of his commission; his
address is coarse and familiar both with inferiors and superiors; to
his political sponsors he is a servile flunkey; by day and by night

he is subject to the paralysis of hush-money, which not infrequently assumes the shape of sly potations and secret sandwiches; he is so "dear" a friend to the gambler that the law must hire instruments other than its own to cause a gambler's arrest; he is so intimate with the rumseller that due notice is afforded that genius of police intentions to suppress him; and sometimes so much is the policeman with the criminal that you cannot distinguish between them, save that the criminal is the more honest of the two! The old proverb, "Set a thief to catch a thief," finds living verification on every corner, and there is no longer any doubt but that the proverb was written for the latitude and longitude of the United States. And his work is performed from no sense of duty, but for what he can make out of it, either in place or cash. He will "stand in" with the thief rather than the law, if there is more to gain by so doing; and he is ever ready to convict the wrong man, if he can thereby secure a point for promotion. The moral law is to him a myth; the local law a piece of polished locust. The people are a set of ninepins, to be knocked down at will, and the authorities the losers, whose duty it is to pay for the game.

"But," opposes the reader, "this is too black a picture; you have made your policeman too much of a villain; I know policemen who are honest, intelligent, faithful, and courteous." So do I; but these are the unhappy exceptions—a few rare exotics amid an acre of weeds. There is nothing I have charged above but what has been proved of the police of the United States during the past year; not of one single man, but of them collectively, of them typically. Read this from the Philadelphia *Record:*

Edward Fish, a gray-haired man, yesterday occupied a seat in the dock of Judge Thayer's court. He pleaded guilty to the larceny of a traveling bag. After the case against the prisoner had been heard, Detective Weyl and several of his brother detectives took the stand and testified that the accused was an old thief, and in support of their allegations produced a photograph from the Rogues' Gallery which bore a striking resemblance to the accused. The case seemed conclusive against Fish, when the District Attorney discovered that on the back of the photograph it was written that the person whose "phiz" was depicted had certain cabalistic marks tattooed on his right arm. Forthwith the prisoner was directed to bare his arm, and a search for the marks was made, when lo! to the surprise and discomfiture of the detectives and the amusement of the general public, not a single tattoo mark was to be found on either arm of the prisoner.

And this, telegraphed to the New York *Herald* from Frederick, Maryland:

An inquest was held here today upon the body of John Israel Groff, who was shot on election day by Police Officer Porter. Some twelve witnesses testified, and the tenor of the entire testimony taken was to the effect that Groff had not been near Porter nor given any provocation for his murderous assault, although there had been a large crowd of colored men around Porter at the time. It seemed to be the general sense of the witnesses that the man Groff had been some distance from Porter at the time the altercation arose, and in Porter's retreat from the maddened crowd he drew near to Groff. After firing a couple of shots into the crowd he turned his pistol directly upon Groff and fired two balls into him. The first, which passed through his left lung and partially severed the main artery, caused his death. Messrs. Maulsby and Nelson, counsel for the prisoner (Porter), were present, but did not take any part in the proceedings. After half an hour's deliberation the jury rendered the following verdict: "That said John Israel Groff came to his death on the morning of November 7, 1882, at Frederick City, Md., from a mortal wound inflicted with a pistol in the hands of Police Officer Charles A. Porter."

And this from the New York *Sun:*

Mr. Edward Scheyer, a maltster, of 462 West Forty-fourth street, obtained from Justice Ford, in the Jefferson Market Police Court, yesterday, a summons for Policeman Eugene Reilly, of Captain Washburn's command, on a charge of violent and uncalled-for assault, for threatening to shoot him, and for unwarranted arrest. Mr. Scheyer last night served the summons upon Policeman Reilly. Mr. Scheyer, who has several respectable businessmen as witnesses, said: "On Thursday night I was walking up Eighth avenue. When near Thirty-fifth street I noticed a man and a woman quarreling, and at the same moment the woman struck the man in the face with her fan. The man, who was in citizen's dress, but whom I now know to be Policeman Eugene Reilly, drew a short club from his pocket and struck the woman several blows, at the same time kicking her. The woman fell and screamed piteously for help. A great crowd was attracted by her screams, and I, with my friends, ran up. As the man kept continually beating the woman, many cried, 'Shame! shame!' The man, who was dragging the woman along the sidewalk in a brutal manner, shouted that he was a policeman, and would arrest anybody who interfered with him. I told him that he should not treat a woman in the manner he was doing. This seemed to drive him fairly crazy, for he let go of her and sprang at me.

" 'I'll take you in, anyway,' he shouted.

"I saw he was drunk, so I simply said: 'Take me in.' Then he put his hand back into his trousers' pocket and drew a pistol, which he put to my head, threatening to blow my head off. The crowd that followed us to the station was greatly excited, and some of those who composed it cried, 'Shame! shame!'

"All the way to the station the man treated me in such a brutal manner that I have not yet recovered from the effects of the assault. Even before the desk, while Sergeant Havens was taking down the complaint, Reilly made a furious assault upon me and tried to shoot me. The pistol was taken from him. Fortunately, Sergeant Havens, who is a cool and gentlemanly man, listened to me patiently and to my witnesses. Then he at once discharged me."

And this from the Chicago *Times:*

A Chicago Police Justice yesterday fined a girl $5 for being alone in the street at 9 o'clock in the evening. She was on her way home from the store where she worked, and had deviated slightly from the straightest route in order to get air and exercise, when a policeman accosted her insultingly. She retorted saucily, and an arrest for spite followed. The magistrate said it was doubtless true that she was entirely respectable, but she deserved punishment for being out unattended after dark.

And this from the Philadelphia *Press:*

> The New York police force of about 2,300 men had over 100 men on trial Wednesday for offenses of varying brutality, from clubbing defenseless women to arresting men for sitting on their own doorsteps. But this did not prevent one of the men on duty from furnishing ground for another complaint by knocking a young woman down. Judging from the proportion of cases to the number of men on duty, about every tenth policeman on New York police beats commits some act of violence every month or two.

There is no need to multiply instances. Those above are from the newspapers of the past six months. The testimony could be furnished to fill hundreds of pages such as this, and the objecting reader should remember that the strength of a chain is the strength of its weakest link.

The police are the eyes, ears, and hands of the law. If the eyes are shortsighted eyes, if the ears are deaf ears, and the hands paralytic hands, what chance has the law for execution? What chance for respect, for value as a deterrent? It has to deal with the sharpest, shrewdest class of citizens in the community. Virtuous citizens are never a match for vicious citizens in energy, ability, or enterprise. The Jay Goulds can always get round the honest man. Herein lies a second charge against the police. In addition to being absolutely incompetent, they are absolutely nonprogressive. The methods of policing employed five-and-forty years ago are their methods today. Where they are not marching to the rear, they are standing still. If they adopt any improvement the suggestion comes from an outsider, not from a police officer; and, what is more discouraging, the police seem to have no ambition to do anything to improve the police systems of the country. The criminal classes are two hundred years ahead of the police in everything indicative of progress. The discoveries of science, the conflict of laws, the triumphs of invention, the carelessness of commerical dealings, are appreciated first by the criminals, last by the police. The skilled forger knows everything about inks, printing, and lithographing; about chemicals and paper; about checks, business forms, and methods. The burglar has minute knowledge of the properties of iron and steel, and understands the temper of metals.

He can tell silver from plate; knows what paper is negotiable and what not; is acquainted with the intricacies of locks; can ascertain by listening to the lock movements on what combination your safe is shut; has studied the power and effect of explosives; the use and strength of anaesthetics; the limits and loopholes of the law. There is little about plates, engraving processes and printing, paper and paper manufacture, that is new to the counterfeiter. The coiner is a machinist and practical metallurgist. The swindler is a student of law. The murderer is a chemist, skilled in the virtues of poisons, and has a profound knowledge of anatomy. And these brilliant, clever, energetic gentlemen arrive in town by the limited express, notify their confederates by telegraph, dispose of their successful villainy by advertisement in the leading newspapers, and retire to the metropolis to enjoy their gains!

Per contra, what do the police know of all the trades and professions of the criminals, or of the progress which they indicate? Nothing. For thirty years and over the police have enjoyed the advantages of the telegraph, and I have yet to learn of a first attempt to secure for important police messages priority over private business. No desire has been manifested to regularly exchange important information between city and city, as it is done in England by a daily official gazette. No systematic effort has been made to suppress the sale of stolen goods by regulating the pawnbroking business. A general of the army would hardly think of placing all his sentries in the middle of his camp. Yet in each of our cities the most illy-protected portions are the outskirts, where a single patrolman is accounted sufficient for ten to fifteen miles of streets. The policeman in England, France, Germany, Spain, Belgium, Austria, and other countries is trained to his duties. Some preparation is made, some care taken, that he shall not enter on his high responsibilities without at least being warned of their nature. He studies invariably all law likely to govern cases in which he will be called upon to act; for a policeman is constantly obliged to decide at a moment's notice law points that take the greatest lawyers in the commonwealth months to wrangle out afterward. What preparation have our policemen for this duty? None. We confide the highest responsibilities, the most vital questions, our property, our lives, to the hands of crass ignorance, and trust to luck for security. Our businessmen repose so much confidence in the police that they employ thousands of private watchmen to

attest it. And we permit them to do so, for we permit most anything. We permit, for instance, any kind of iniquity to be practiced
by private detectives. We even allow them to work up evidence
against the government, against the very authority that licenses
their existence. And nowhere are there signs of change. Chicago
enjoys one jot of progress—a police wagon. Boston made a move
in the right direction some years ago, and organized a Board of
Police Commissioners. But the infant was soon throttled by political influence, and is dead. "Philadelphia," says her Mayor in his
annual message, "has the finest force in the country," and the
force must be excused when respectable citizens are clubbed,
because it is only done when the police are under the stress of
arduous labor. Is it supposable that a policeman would club a
respectable man over the head if he had a month's time to think
about it? The evil is that whenever there is the least strain the
chain snaps, and some one else is hurried away to the hospital or
the morgue; while heart disease, apoplexy, and fits are mistaken
for drunkenness, and the cells of the stationhouses are filled with
dying men.

This is the police problem; this the picture before us: Incompetence, ignorance, brutality, and corruption. From whence the deliverance? It is idle to hope for anything out of the regeneration
of political parties. That day is too far off. Policemen must and will
remain the approximation prizes of political lotteries. The power
of the police is too great, too valuable to be surrendered by the
politician. As a menace or a reward it is all potent. It is usually the
extent of the ward-worker's ambition, and no political manager
ever yet had the least intention of abandoning the ward-worker
or his desires. Relief from this quarter, the only quarter it can now
come from, is impossible. A Chinese wall of selfishness is in the
way. Whence then the deliverance, the solution of the police problem? In my judgment from the editorial rooms of the great daily
newspapers, in the formation and operation in every large newspaper office of a Bureau of Criminal Investigation.

It is not necessary to detail here the methods that would be
employed in the organization of the bureau; they would be understood only by newspapermen. Suffice it to say the bureau would
be organized with a chief and the necessary number of assistants.
All would be able, gentlemanly journalists, with some taste and
decided abilities for their work. The first step to obtain the neces-

sary powers would be swearing in the men as special officers without pay, which would give them the authority to make an arrest. The want of this authority has threatened the defeat of justice in dozens of instances. Mr. John Norris, of the Philadelphia *Record,* when he had unearthed the bogus-diploma doctor, Buchanan, was obliged to take an officer with him to Detroit, merely that the officer—otherwise of no earthly use—might make a legal arrest. The Boston *Herald* representative who captured Chastine Cox followed that murderer for a mile-and-a-half on Boston streets without seeing a policeman, and was obliged to leave Cox unwatched in order that the authority necessary to cause his apprehension might be summoned. But no one will dispute me that the power to arrest should be conferred on the ability to detect. After the power of arrest had been secured for the members of the bureau, they should by study and examination prepare to quality as notaries public or justices of the peace, and such laws should be passed as would confer on them not only the authority to take a sworn deposition, but in cases of crime the power to compel one, as have the "judges of instruction" in France. On passing the examination prescribed for admission to the bar, the bureau reporters would receive a license—say yearly—from the state executive, which license should be indorsed by the executives of all states in which the reporter would be likely to go. This authority to take sworn depositions in murder and other cases, depositions taken before the witnesses to the crime had opportunity to confer with each other, or read the morning papers and make ready a tale of deception and delusion, would prove of enormous, inestimable value to the machinery of American justice. It would increase the number of punished cases at least thirty percent, and it is easily appreciable how much more valuable would be the depositions taken by keen-eyed reporters, educated to the law and having professional pride to sharpen their wits, than unsworn statements obtained by uneducated policemen, whose first care is to ascertain the political and social affiliations of the accused. Also, how much clearer and intelligent would be the reporter's testimony than is that of the policeman, who usually appears in court with a sergeant or lieutenant as his prompter and coach. Additionally, the reporters would be well read in criminal jurisprudence, qualified in local law, posted in the history of crime, and up in chemistry, mechanics, anatomy, and the habits of the criminal classes. There would be no attempt to do a general police business, nor make an investigation of petty misdemeanors. But there would be a most energetic, determined effort to uproot all great and peculiar crimes, and to detect and punish the leaders in those fearful mysteries that nowadays occur only to be added to the catalogue of unsolved horrors. It is not necessary to argue the ability of the newspaper men to detect where the police fail. The files of the daily papers will show that for the last five years all of the great crimes that have been detected have been through the active agency of a reporter; that is, the reporter has furnished *the detecting link* in the chain of detection. And this has been done while the reporter has been handicapped with the silence of the authorities, to whom, of course, has been accessible all official information. The striking triumph of the Detroit *Post and Tribune* in proving a man guilty of murder after his acquittal of the charge in a court of justice is proof of quite recent date. And every journalist is aware that if a great crime is committed, say at 6:00 P.M., the newspaper which closes its columns at 3:00 A.M. next day will, ninety times out of a hundred, contain more information concerning the affair when it reaches police headquarters at 7:00 A.M. than is known to the police at that hour. The late Henry Pawling Ross, President Judge of Montgomery County, Pennsylvania, had a murder case before him last year, and during the examination he threatened to commit two private detectives—who had the case in charge—as accessories after the fact, *because they refused to give information to the reporters.* On being asked about the matter he said to me that reporters had come to be a far more efficient agency in the detection of crime than the police, and that he held it a principle of law that no one should be allowed to place obstacles in the path of justice.

Objections will at once be offered to my ideas. I shall be told that "the reporter, already a necessary nuisance, if given legal license in addition to that he now assumes, will ruin every man in the community; that he will become the terror of the town; that all kinds of villainies will be practiced for the sake of sensations and in the contests of rivalry; that social blackmail of gigantic proportions will follow any such social innovation." Such objections are not worthy of serious men. The commonest, most dissolute reporter will compare favorably with the average policeman, and in comparison with some of "the finest" the reporter is a revelation of civilization. But the trusts of the Bureau of Criminal Investigation would be in the hands of gentlemen and the best reporters. Place one of these beside any police commissioner or chief of police in the land, and the newspaper man will "double discount" the other in every quality that makes a useful citizen and a man. The inaccuracy of newspapers today in regard to criminal matters is not the inaccuracy of the staff editors, but of inexperienced reporters denied official information, or furnished by the police with false news. And all other objections to my ideas will come from those who have something to cover up, who fear publicity, who are afraid to let the light of day fall upon the shadowy pages of their own story. It is, however, an axiom of our everyday life, an axiom that has been fashioned by the grinding of facts, that publicity never hindered the course of justice. Publicity is the only thing crime fears. Without question, publicity in uncompleted police cases will generally interfere with police operations *as now conducted!* But the fiercest light that beats upon a throne, if turned full upon any case of criminal procedure properly conducted, will not cast so much as a shadow upon the path of justice. I defy proof to the contrary. No one knows better than the journalist when to publish and when not to. Every day some case of rascality is disclosed that was discovered, worked up, and exposed by the newspaper, from the very columns of which the police receive their first intimation of the "crookedness."

As opposed to these empty and any other objections are the great overmatching advantages that bureaus of criminal investigation would confer upon the community. They are many and appreciable. True and full testimony concisely given in court I have mentioned. Then bribery, the garroter of justice, would be impossible. What a tremendous step forward this would be! If a criminal should succeed in silencing a single bureau he would have as much to fear as before. He could not silence all the bureaus, and, even supposing every bureau was purchasable, it would not be possible to do so before some one had printed the rascality. And no reporter would dare accept a bribe, for some one else would get the news. Bribery impossible, the chief gate to freedom would be inexorably closed to the criminal. Further, the police would be compelled to attend to their duties in self-defense. Politics could no longer interfere to save the reputation of a villain and cheat the prison of its due. Testimony would be freed from the handcuffs of dishonesty, and would approximate to what it ought to be. The false incarceration of criminals would be put a stop to, as every man's case would be impartially presented. No one would dare interfere, because he would read of it the next day. The cause of detection would be so materially advanced that punishment for crime would acquire a measure of certainty; and if punishment were a certainty crime would be lessened one-half. The country districts would be furnished with the best detective talent; not that routine intelligence that now goes there in the guise of a city officer, and who proceeds to work out a solution by the old-established rules, but that talent which brings energy, ability and common sense together to effect a result. The city victims of the criminal would more readily do their whole duty when victimized and more generously advance the cause of law and order, for they could trust where now they fear. The publication of criminal acts would be more accurate and less sensational, and the machinery to detect villainy now in existence would be trebled in efficiency, force, and purpose. The newspaper would realize more nearly a part of its mission, and the community would attain a more healthy, progressive growth.

Incidentally, too, the bureau would rid us, in inducing primary legal reforms, of that terrible barnacle the coroner, a worthless, witless individual, whose sole function has come to be the raising of obstacles to justice. It is, indeed, a satire on our day and generation that in this nineteenth century it takes six able-bodied men to find out that "the deceased came to his death at the hands of some person to the jury unknown." For the last twenty years the American coroner has contented himself with ruining every case that has come into his pestilential hands. Said the Philadelphia *Times* the other day:

> Dr. Cadwallader reported at the inquest yesterday that there was sufficient reason for the belief that the beheaded, dismembered body found in the Delaware, off Shackamaxon street, on Tuesday, was that of a woman about five feet five inches high and twenty-five years old. The verdict "found dead" disposed of the mystery.

Do we want mysteries disposed of in that way? Is this our duty to our fellowman? Is it creditable to us that we permit an annual waste of many hundreds of thousands of dollars merely that a coroner and six men shall tell us that some poor, murdered soul was "found dead!"

I will not argue further nor touch on more of the many mushroom iniquities that stand between the people and the blessing of honest, respected law. I have advanced an idea that in some office like that of the New York *Herald,* where there is both courage and money, may be molded into a force for the benefit of the people. Though I have presented the matter somewhat sketchily, it may perhaps be taken up, for it deserves serious consideration, and I trust, at no distant day, bureaus of criminal investigation will be matters of American history.

Chapter 16

Carrying Handguns

We recently commented in these columns upon the vicious habit of carrying concealed weapons, and urged that public sentiment should emphatically assert itself against the practice. But, inasmuch as our police are accustomed to go armed with revolvers, it may be questioned whether the public can be induced to look upon the habit with due severity, so long as this example is before them. It will be claimed that the police are compelled to go armed as a necessary protection, but this is by no means evident. It is certain that their example is followed by many who otherwise would not carry weapons; the police, in fact, give a sort of legal sanction to a custom that has very notably increased since it was thought necessary to permit these guardians of the peace to adopt it. The public have become familiarized with the idea of murderous weapons, and one may note a continual increase of crime in which this weapon is used. If we are going to arrest the user of the pistol, we must begin with the police—or, rather, we should begin with very rigid laws against the practice of carrying the pistol, the police as well as others to be made amenable to them. The neces-

Reprinted from *Appleton's Journal,* 4 (September 24, 1870), 382. Title added by Editor.

sity of the pistol as a means of protection for the police we utterly
deny. It was not found necessary in former years; it is not found
necessary in English cities. We rarely or never hear of the pistol
serving an important aid in the protection of the officers of the law,
but we do often hear of its use under circumstances that ought to
excite our liveliest indignation.

A short time since a crowd was pursuing a fugitive through the
streets of Brooklyn, crying vociferously, "Stop thief!" A policeman
joined in the pursuit, and, soon finding that the fugitive was likely
to escape, drew his pistol and fired. The ball took effect, and the
man, staggering a few steps up a side passageway, fell, and almost
instantly expired. Now, the killing of this fugitive, in the language
of a contemporary, "to all intents and purposes amounted to the
infliction of capital punishment upon a man not tried, for an
offence not specified, by an executive not commissioned, in obedience to an act never passed." Let us consider well the magnitude
of this indictment. Let us understand clearly that this surrender
into the hands of one man of almost all the functions of legal
government, is the erection of an absolute and formidable despotism, which, if permitted to go on, will in time place us all at the
mercy of a body of men, selected nominally to protect the community, but in administration constituting themselves the law, and
the judges of the law, in regard to every one accused or suspected.
The right of punishment should never be lodged in the hands of
the police at all, let alone the right of life. It is not only infamous
that a pistol should be fired in our crowded streets, to the great
danger of the innocent, but it is monstrous that a power so summary and formidable should be exercised by any person without
due process, due formality, and absolute sanction of the law. And
yet, when we arm our police, we give them the right to use their
weapons. When we place the pistol in their hands, we instruct
them that they may in one single breath, as it were, suspect, indict,
judge, sentence, and execute. We cannot excuse ourselves by saying that the pistol is to be used only in extreme instances. We
permit these men to be the judges of the occasions when it may
be used. If we assure them they may kill us in one case, they will
be certain to extend the privilege to kill in another. To assume that
they may kill in any instance, is to lodge in their hands a tremendous power which no free community should for an instant permit
to exist outside of its courts. A policeman may do in self-defence

just what any other man may do; but if, in the exercise of his office, simply in the performance of the functions of his place, he kills, then his killing is and should be considered a crime, answerable to law like other crimes.

If it is necessary, let us double our police force. Let us be sure our means are sufficient to protect the peace without resorting to means to accomplish it which render subordinates of the law higher than the law—which give to inferior officers of the law a power which is as summary, as formidable, as dangerous, as the most absolute despotism known.

Chapter 17

Needed Reforms in Prison Management

Z. R. Brockway

Reforms are needed. The jails of today are, with here and there an exception, substantially what Howard in the eighteenth century found jails to be. The fault is largely due to construction. Jails on the "Pennsylvania Plan," supplying separate confinement for each prisoner, will provide the needed reforms for jails. Prisons of later date, designed not only for detention but punishment as well, have scarcely been improved, though of prison associations and boards there are many, and prison congresses, state, national and international, have been held, with their valuable discussions and issue of reports. Prisons for reformation are still of later origin, but they do not reform in any such general and efficient way as to perceptibly affect the volume of recorded crimes. Given the number of the population to the square mile, with absence of war, pestilence, famine, or monetary revulsions, it is said the annual aggregate of crimes in a district may be as accurately foretold as

Reprinted from Z. R. Brockway, "Needed Reforms in Prison Management," in *North American Review*, 137 (July, 1883), 40–48.

the death rate of a people can be calculated by Carlisle's tables. Then, there is abroad a popular demand for reforms; the communistic sentiment of the time calls for them, hoping for pecuniary benefits, and the politician echoes the cry for partisan effect, while the press and the populace repeat it from motives selfish or sentimental as the case may be. Finally, the thoughtful, the philanthropic and public spirited, saddened at sight of so much sin and alarmed at the growth of crime, ask for an advance in both the theory and practice of "crime treatment," that crimes may be diminished and criminals reclaimed. With so much room for reforms, the general demand cannot properly be put aside; there must be underneath it all a common source of good impulse that needs only to be rightly directed.

The first great need in this matter is a better sentiment, among prison governors and the public, as to the true purpose of prisons and treatment of criminals for crime. There is an almost universal demand for retaliation, or at best a retributing of evil for evil. What the public sense for the time approves is named justice, but that is often a misnomer: for, under the name of justice, injustice is inflicted upon criminals, and through improper release of confirmed criminals, before or after conviction, society is unjustly dealt with. This popular demand, as expressed in our criminal laws and their administration, is the bane of good government, either encourages the criminal or consigns him to degradation, and tends to confirm rather than cure the criminal traits of character. Could this current sentiment be replaced with the passionless demand that every criminal when once fairly convicted shall be reasonably cured of his criminality as the only condition of freedom again, the primary requisite for reformed prison management would be reached. Neither punishment for the sake of it, nor pardon for the pleasure of it, but punishment and pardon, either or both, when promotive of reformation—that is the only real security society can have from known criminals. Suitable laws and systems of prison management based on such a sentiment will supply the second needed reform, namely: A motive operating powerfully upon criminals to cause them to relinquish their practices and return to regular industry with right use of citizenship.

An analysis of human motives brings us always to avoidance of pain or pursuit of pleasure as the active principle in conduct; but since one man's pain is another's pleasure, and by the marvelous

instinctive adjustment to environment the pain of today sometimes becomes the pleasure of tomorrow, it is simply impossible
by any schedule of predetermined penalties to supply for the mass
of criminals an adequate deterrent or reformative motive. The
history of crimes and punishments throughout the civilized world
sustains the statement of Beccaria, that the public mind becomes
habituated to penalties, so that in the space of a hundred years the
gibbet terrifies no more than fines or imprisonment. No doubt the
innate love of liberty and natural repugnance to the privations of
imprisonment are facts with all men, and warrant the general
application of imprisonment for crime. It is not possible, however,
and, therefore, not properly the province of legislation, to precisely prescribe either the pains or duration of imprisonment.
These, within due bounds, should be left to the prison governors,
to be determined and varied from time to time for reformation,
according to the idiosyncrasy and ever-changing subjective state
of the criminal in confinement. Prison governors thus charged
with the protection of society from fresh crimes by criminals,
through their cure or continued restraint, are clothed with great
powers, and should be held to strict accountability. They must not
be trammeled by the meddlesome interference of partisanship,
whether political or religious. Due protection from criminals, in-
volving as it does their reformation or detention in custody, naturally necessitates a systematic if not positively a scientific
treatment, which is only practicable when the prisons are on a
plane above, beyond, and outside of partisanship or prejudice.
Therefore, the third needed reform is here stated to be the removal of prison management entirely out of the sphere of partisan
politics and denominationalism.

Coming now to the more practical reforms, which may be
wrought at will when the three above-named general conditions
exist, the first to be named is a classification of criminals immured.
There has sprung up a kind of natural separation of different
classes of criminals, but it is imperfect and ineffective. The sexes
in prison are uniformly separated; unless there is an exceptional
and exceptionable county jail where the sexes are allowed to mingle, the principle of sex separation in prison is usually accepted.
In some of the states where the color line remains, the separation
of whites and blacks is necessary or politic; in European or nothern
prisons it is unnecessary. The separation of youthful from mature

criminals is conceded to be serviceable. The very plausible idea that prisoners should be classified "according to the character and circumstances of the crime" is fallacious, if the object is to protect the novice from the contamination of experienced criminals; for it is a common fact that first offenders are guilty of high crimes and habitual criminals commit venial offenses. The technical title of the crime is not a sure index of the offender's character. There are, of course, professional criminals addicted to particular crimes that call for and develop distinctive traits, but comparatively few criminals are "professionals," and even these turn aside sometimes to crimes of another grade; while all grades of crime attract and engage the youthful and inexperienced. The distinctions of the criminal statutes are based mainly on the amount of damage done, which is often determined by accident. The same hand and intent may govern the harmless thrust and drive home the deadly stiletto; larceny is of one degree or another according to the opportunity to steal; the burglar breaks and enters usually without thought or knowledge of the statutory definitions determining the grade of his crime. For purposes of classification, conduct in prison, as conduct is generally rated by prison officials, is not a satisfactory criterion, but it is possible to make it so. Under a prison system that gives play to the natural impulses of the prisoner when in contact with conditions somewhat analogous to free society, the fitness for free life may be very accurately ascertained. The experienced prison manager must remember surprises when his good man in prison has gone "to the dogs" on his release, while the troublesome customer has turned out well. All these facts of sex, color, age, crime, and conduct may have an influence in classifying criminals; but none of them, separately considered, constitutes the true basis. It is the real diversity of character among them, to be discerned after the wisest scrutiny and fullest opportunity to apply tests from time to time. The scrutiny must include somewhat of the ancestral history, much of the early environment, and a careful personal examination of the criminal himself as to his physical quality and condition, his mental capacity and culture or unculture, and also his moral susceptibility and his sensitiveness or apathy in view of his crime and its consequences.

Classification may be effected by a general separation of prisoners into two divisions immediately on conviction, either by the sentence of the court or the central governing authority of the prisons themselves, the susceptible to one division, the apparently incorrigible to another, subject to transfer afterward by the prison governors from one division to the other to perfect this general classification. The prisoners of a state may thus be separated in different prison establishments or in a single prison. In the division of susceptibles, the ruling aim in administration would naturally be reformation and early restoration to liberty; and for the other, the incorrigibles, a more rigorous *régime* would be provided, and probably a longer period of detention would be required. The further classification within the two general divisions and in each separate establishment thereof should be into three grades without separation; that is to say, with limited and supervised association, and then progress toward liberation to be so conditioned that it shall involve of necessity on the part of the prisoner an actual progress of reformation.

Another much needed practical reform is the compulsory education of prisoners. It is high time the farce were ended of placing criminals in durance, to be worked simply for the profits of their labor, preached to and soon released, unchanged, upon the community. There is no protection without reformation, and there is no reformation without education. The criminal must outgrow his criminality, and the growth can be, and, therefore, should be, forced if necessary. Education, using the term in its broad and comprehensive sense, is at once the means, and the process, and no other word so well expresses the product we call reformation. It involves training to proper self-regulation and to efficient industrial application, and at least an increase of mental and moral illumination. The present practice of releasing criminals without improved impulses, unfitted for and without access to decent associations, without visible means of support, whether of money, occupation, or capacity; but, on the other hand, as is too often the case, with an added impulse and power for evil, is both absurd and dangerous. Said a convict: "We reached New York at evening with what remained of the five dollars given at the door of the prison when released that day. I had a merry night of it, and was immediately on the road again."

Mr. George W. Cable estimates at a quarter of a million the exconvicts abroad in the United States, of which there must be in New York full twenty thousand. The Secretary of State reports, for 1881, the names of eleven hundred and twenty-nine convicts dismissed during that year from the three long-term prisons alone, while of felons and misdemeanants both it is safe to say that there are ten thousand of them annually emptied from the prisons into society in the same state. The country is overrun with released criminals, carrying to the youth of the classes they mingle with the contamination of their own criminal character. Let the prisons be renovated. Put away retribution, restrain sentimentalism; sentence criminals to be restrained or reformed as they may elect or be able; then wield this mighty motive, their love of liberty, for their education until they properly discern between right and wrong as principles of action, until the better impulses instinctively preponderate, and sufficient strength of mind and will is developed to consummate the good choice when tempted to evil. And, for those that will not or, unfortunately, cannot receive such culture, let them remain restrained to such extent and in such manner as best protects society from their further crimes.

The prisoner put through this training should, on his return to society, have a fair chance to build himself up, and it is the duty as well as the wise policy of the state, through proper officers, to see that he has it. It will be a most salutary reform when the prisoner, previous to his final release from legal restraint, is completely rehabilitated. He must be actually introduced into suitable permanent employment, surrounded with reasonably good influences, and should be officially supervised until the habit is formed of saving from his earnings, serving faithfully, and properly behaving himself in ordinary society. Passing, while in confinement, through a graduated course of training, so conditioned that actual progress of improvement must be made, he is, on reaching a point of probable safe release, at once restored to the rights, the privileges, and the obligations, too, of good citizenship, to be under observation until established in well doing and readjusted to current affairs. He is thus protected from the temptations of idleness, friendlessness, and unrestrained liberty; at the same time, through the fact of his legal liabilities persisting for a time, his newfound purposes and powers are stimulated, and society retains some guarantee against further criminal conduct. This is not the English ticket-of-leave system, though somewhat similar. There is an important difference, for the English system involves police supervision, keeping the prisoner within the category of suspects and in contact with the governmental machinery for the detection and conviction of criminals; while this is parole under state guardianship, and he is responsible to officers who seek his security in a right use of liberty, instead of detectives, district attorneys, and the directors of penitentiaries who seek his conviction and confinement.

In the disciplinary government of prisoners, for individual treatment the *en masse* plan needs to be substituted. Officers must be better informed of the differentia of criminals as a class and from each other. The Spanish writer, Señor Arenal, says:

> In the prisoner who steals, two things are observable—the thief and the man. The thief constitutes the diseased part, the man the sound part. No two are alike; so that two men breaking the law under the same external circumstances may enter upon imprisonment with impressions totally different. The malady may be the same, but the internal resources to vanquish it will greatly vary.

Failing to perceive this, outraged society sometimes crushes the man with the criminal, or fosters the criminal with sentimentalism lavished upon the man. Prison officers, seeing only the criminal, constantly antagonizing him, conserve not the man until manliness from disuse dies out, while the criminal by the activity of opposition thrives and becomes strong. These diverse qualities, differently combined, discoverable in every criminal, are of necessity to be treated in conjunction: to repress the one and develop the other is the process of reformation; evil cannot be cured with evil; not until evil is overcome of good is any man reformed. To discern the one from the other in the same individual requires a competent, thoughtful, interested mind constantly in contact with criminals; and when this personal work is properly done by the chief officer of a prison, he will be as accessible to all as is the principal of a school or manager of a manufactory. Then will better results be wrought, and vain will be the search for neglect and cruelty often publicly charged and investigated.

Since imprisonment is for protection, the disciplinary management should be not punitive but remedial; prison punishments for correction only, never for retribution, give perfection of discipline in proportion to the wisdom and skill of the governors. Legislative restrictions and public accusations, revealing as they do a lack of confidence, often necessitate severities that would not otherwise be required. The limits of vested authority in this matter must be broad: good discipline means the voluntary cheerful obedience of prisoners with the least of punishments. The favorable conditions for it are:

1.—Power vested in the managers.
2.—Power wisely used for remedial ends alone.
3.—Power, in action, closely scrutinized.

The demagogic demand for reform in the industrial employment of prisoners does not, judging from the reasons publicly given, entitle it to space here for discussion. That prisoners confined under sentence must be employed, nobody will deny; their employment mainly at mechanical pursuits is a necessity if they are to be reclaimed, and also almost a custodial disciplinary and pecuniary necessity if irreclaimable. If, then, prisoners are to be employed, and at mechanical work, it matters little, as prisons now are, whether it be by the contract system or on the public account plan. The latter may be made more favorable to reformation in prisons where that object is rationally sought. There is no positive difference as relates to labor and mercantile competition. The amount of income to be derived by the state will be greater or less from either system, according to circumstances; the proportion of income does not inhere in either. Under classification, as previously described, the industries of the incorrigible division would be mainly for production of income, and naturally on the contract system, though not necessarily so. The real incorrigibles constitute less than one-half of the prisoners of the state, so that there would be at once a diminution of convict contract labor equal to full fifty percent of the whole, which, with wise selection of industries for them, ought, when they are earning their own subsistence, as they could easily do, to satisfy all who now sincerely oppose the convict contract system.

The susceptible class should and would be employed at a greater variety of trades, including some of the higher mechanic arts; employed on public account or under a modified form of contract, as by the piece or process, or on the principle of partitioning the profits of each separate industry between the state and expert managers, whose office would mainly be to prepare the prisoners for success in business when released. This last is the really needed reform in prison industries, namely: that the purpose shall be to place the prisoner on release in such a position in society as he would or should have filled had he refrained from crime and been a good citizen. That it were better for all if the criminal had found active, honorable place in legitimate industry, all must admit; it follows, then, that it is best for all that he be fitted while imprisoned for such place. No fair-minded man, manufacturer, mechanic, or laborer, will object to such employment for such an end. To classify and employ prisoners in this way will go far toward settling the difficulties that now environ the prison labor question.

Yet another reform is needed. It is in the ministrations of religion to prisoners. Reform its partisanship; it is too often factitious or feeble, and is fragmentary. The religious influencing of prisoners must be made a part of a unified system of their general treatment; it properly belongs to the educational function. Because the mass of criminals in prison are below the point of development where ordinary religious influences can lodge, a preliminary preparation of cultivation is absolutely necessary: obstacles to the apprehension as well as reception of religious ideas and benign spiritual energies must be cleared away. The religious development of any people is dependent on varied social influences; the wise religious guide brings us to the recognition of religion in our practical life: so the teacher or religion to prisoners needs to harmonize his work with other departments of the prison administration, and adapt his instructions to the particular state and condition of the criminal. There is room for improvement in the time and manner of such ministrations. A systematic course of teaching should supplement simple exhortation, and a steady pressure of truth and moral means with (rather than against) the industrial and purely educational efforts, should replace desultory and sentimental methods. The great mass of first offenders may be reformed, and but a small proportion of prisoners are irreclaimable when with right means and methods reclamation is really sought. Every reformatory prison should reproduce the conditions of free life as near as may be; the requirements of good citizenship should be enforced upon prisoners until they show their purpose and ability to comply with them when released.

There are, then, three classes of reforms to be brought about by these several familiar agencies: first, separate confinement in jails for all prisoners therein, the creating of a better public sense of the true purpose of imprisonment, and the removal of prisons from all partisan interference—these to be brought about by agitation and suitable legislation; second, the classification of prisoners, their education while in prison, and their complete rehabilitation when released, to be accomplished by the general governing administration of prisons with suitable legislation; third, the industrial and remedial treatment, with thorough preparatory industrial and moral training.

Some who read this paper will live to see such a prison system generally adopted. Its feasibility is fully confirmed by the success of present experiments. With the reforms here named, crime will feel the force of repression, its recorded aggregate will diminish, or at least its present rank growth will be stayed.

Chapter 18

The Rationale
of the Opposition
to Capital Punishment

E. S. Nadal

... There is one thing, at least, which this age has learned to do: it can pity. The change which has come over us, by whatever adjective it may be described, is none the less a fact which it is necessary to accept, and with which it is idle to expostulate. It may be asked, now, what has the sentimental as distinguished from the experimental opposition to capital punishment to say for itself. It is plain that hanging is "impossible." We need not call it a "relic of the dark ages"; it is simply *passé*. As a means of punishment in good working order, it has been rendered impracticable. Society cannot be kept up to it; the public is generally very glad to sneak out or to cheat itself out of an execution, if it can. But every now and then, say once in two years, murders occur very rapidly, the newspapers become vehement and the governors inexorable. At

Excerpted from E. S. Nadal, "The Rationale of the Opposition to Capital Punishment," in *North American Review,* 116 (January, 1873), 138–150.

such a time any man under sentence of death will be likely to suffer; but the public attention will soon be diverted, the pendulum will swing back. A permanent reform in the direction of rigor and thoroughness, however much it may be desired, is simply out of the question. We must either stop executions at once, or go on hanging in our slack, inefficient manner, until the executions stop themselves. The opponents of the death penalty, knowing it to be "impossible" and useless, and necessarily slovenly and capricious in its administration, have a right to take its horribleness into account as a reason for its immediate discontinuance. The great mass of people, the country through, I suppose, hold the question in abeyance; most men who have strong opinions upon the subject are opposed to executions. And yet we go on hanging people in this absentminded, mechanical manner, because we seem to find no appropriate place to stop. We condone the few executions that take place with the reflection that these are to be the last of them. But this does not make it a bit better for the men who are hanged. On the contrary, it must be particularly trying to be executed under the present state of things. An intelligent culprit must reflect bitterly that all this altered public sentiment goes for naught. The compunctions of the sheriff and the sympathy of the newspaper reporters rather aggravate the case. No man can do more than die, nor could have done any more in the days before Sir Samuel Romilly. He is to be put to death just like any old-time malefactor who never dreamed of such luxuries as the public petitions for his reprieve, the condolence of the clergy, and the tears of the sheriff. I do not intend in this paper to consider the question of the expediency of hanging. There are half a dozen facts one may count on one's fingers which go far towards proving its retention unnecessary. A great empire like Russia does without it; commonwealths like Michigan and Wisconsin have abolished it, and do not return to it; while its abolition has succeeded in many places, I have yet to hear of a case in which it has been tried and failed; if we try it and fail, twenty-four hours' legislation will put us back where we are. These points I merely name in passing; my object is to show that hanging is a very extraordinary and terrible thing. I do not oppose it, let me here remark, because it is terrible; but I say that because it is terrible we should see to it that there is some terrible necessity for it. I wish to remind the reader how strange a thing it is to be hanged. I wish to point out a few of the accidents of capital executions, and to describe and examine some impressions that control our own thinking about them.

One is struck by the caprice and inequality seen everywhere in the administration of the capital sentence. I have referred to the fact that the public mind is not very lofty and solemn in its thinking upon this subject. I have said that it continues to hang because it has not definitely decided not to hang, and that it administers this awful punishment in an "absentminded and mechanical" manner. It would seem the height of levity and sacrilege to lay hands in such a frame of mind upon the mysteries of death and the future state. It would be especially dreadful for men to bring into this thing the shiftlessness, haste, and triviality they exhibit in their ordinary concerns. However they may feel towards the general question, they must at least act with circumspection and firmness. Putting aside graver matters for the present, let us see whether capital punishment is administered with that dignity and equality we should expect.

The mere fact that a man who is hanged in one part of the country should escape in another seems indecorous. In some states, Wisconsin and Michigan, for instance, there is no capital punishment. A man is hanged in New Jersey for killing his mistress's paramour; while a person in Michigan who might murder and horribly mangle a whole congregation, pastor, Sunday school, and infant class, would get off with imprisonment for life. This is a mere accidental difference in state laws, but there are other social differences which are more radical and necessary. The farther you go west the harder it is to condemn a murderer to death. Capital punishment exists by law both in Leavenworth and in Boston. Yet in many cases where the same crime has been committed, the convicted man would suffer in Boston and escape in Leavenworth.

Then, again, culprits are hanged at certain times who would not be hanged at others. When murder has been very general and people are angry or alarmed, the criminal will have less chance of escape than when the community is unconscious of insecurity. When two men are to suffer at the same time in the same state, the likelihood of commutation of the sentence of either by the governor is slight. Both Twitchell and Eaton, who were convicted of murder a few years since in Philadelphia, would perhaps have escaped death, had their crimes fallen at different times. Both were convicted on circumstantial evidence. Twitchell's murder was an exceptionally brutal one, but he was defended by a very able, influential, and indefatigable man. Eaton's guilt was not so great nor so clear. The governor was one of those imitators of Brutus who think it an impressive and distinguished thing to hang somebody. He would not have dared to reprieve both, though he might not have hanged Eaton had Eaton been alone. But as he was pressed very energetically in Twitchell's behalf, it was the natural, though unconscious, concession to that gentleman's friends to hang Eaton.

Again, much would depend upon the mere accident of a governor's personal character, whether he was a clearheaded, firm man, or a soft, weak man, or an obstinate, conceited, heartless man. There is no doubt that popularity will be considered by governors in this as in other matters. Pardons are supposed to be unpopular, and governors, with that sensibility to indefinite alarm common to officeholders, are often afraid to interfere. An executive who was a candidate for reelection would be less apt to commute a sentence of death than one who had no intention of taking office again. Just before an election he would be particularly careful not to confront what was or what he would think to be an offended public sentiment. Here the reader may think me inconsistent. I say that pardons may make governors unpopular, and yet I say that most people are opposed to capital punishment. This apparent contradiction is explained by the fact that people feel very differently towards hanged and unhanged criminals. We do not clearly enough perceive that criminals must either be hanged or not hanged—that there is no middle course. We would like some arrangement by which both things could be done. Accordingly, when a murderer is reprieved, our nerves are not shocked by the spectacle of his execution, while we may satisfy our sense of justice by blaming and ridiculing the governor who reprieves him. It is true, also, that we dislike the mere idea of any mitigation of penalty for a convicted murderer. Were there no hanging, there would be no idea of mitigation when a criminal was sent to the penitentiary for life. It would be satisfactory to know that the culprit had suffered all the punishment we had it in our power to inflict. As the case stands at present, governors are wise in thinking that too many commutations of the death penalty will make them unpopular and ridiculous. The question of personal popularity will enter into the consideration of the act, along with the questions of justice and public policy.

•   •   •

There is yet a grosser inequality than any of these. We cannot shut our eyes to the fact that social position makes a difference. A man cannot easily be hanged who has a very good position in the community. It has been done in one or two cases, but the circumstances were peculiar. The causes of this immunity of the respectable people are twofold: first, a lack of thoroughness and tenacious adherence to principle among our people; secondly, the inability of the immense comfortable middle class of the country to bring distinctly before them the sufferings of the very low. That young ladies who go to tea parties and have accomplishments should lose a brother or father in such a way seems very dreadful. We do not so easily conceive the miseries of people who live in uncarpeted hovels. Another explanation is to be found in the *inertia* of an impression which once gets into the mind. That a man is fortunate is a reason with us why he should continue to be so; that he is unsuccessful is also a reason why he should continue to be so.

Republicans as we are, I believe there is no country where respectability claims so many immunities, and has them so instinctively accorded, as in America. If a man of wealth and respectability is put in the penitentiary, it is very difficult to keep him there; not only because of the pressure brought to bear for his pardon, but because of the widespread commiseration his family receives from the public. To hang such a person would be next to impossible. If he committed some very exceptional crime, he might be hanged; but for the same offence for which many a Hans and Patrick would suffer he would go free. Yet the root of this is not so much to be found in any particular respect for "good circumstances," as in our peculiar ability to pity. And we pity the lawyers and clergymen, and the well-to-do people of middle life, more than the Wares and the Eatons, because we know more about them, and have a more vivid notion of the sufferings such a death would entail upon them and their friends.

Another inequality is in the method of administering punishment. Some people are much better hanged than others. This may seem to be a fine point, but I am not so sure there is nothing in it. Men have always laid great stress upon the manner of execution. There must be as much difference between good and bad hanging as between most entirely distinct ways of inflicting the death penalty. A man who dies at once is certainly more fortunate than one who is compelled to suffer through some minutes of strangulation. In England, not more than a year ago, a culprit who had not the good luck to be one of Calcraft's patients, had his head torn entirely off. The hanging all over England is done by Calcraft, who goes about the country from place to place, wherever his services are needed. But in America the distances are too great for such an officer to get over; and in remote localities they have to rely upon the best amateur talent the neighborhood can improvise. Hanging in our cities, I suppose, is pretty well done; in the country it is often very badly done. This seems to constitute an advantage for the urban over the rural malefactor.

•   •   •

. . . If murders are many, it proves that hanging does not prevent them; if murders are few, there is no need of resorting to such extreme means in dealing with them. We have no experience which shows that murders increase when hanging is abolished. We have the histories of states and empires that have done away with it, and do not return to it. Its enemies are practical; its friends, *a priori* and theoretical. The thing itself is very horrible, and the time has come to try if we cannot do without it. . . .

Chapter 19

Preventable Causes of Poverty
Henry Dwight Chapin

One of the gravest problems today confronting society is found in the wide extension of great poverty—in the fact that a large number make a pitiful failure in the sharp struggle for subsistence. Many and diverse are the panaceas offered to remedy this state of affairs, but very few are based upon a correct appreciation and knowledge of the operation of natural law.

Undoubtedly the trend of social development is toward industrial democracy, where natural inherited, together with acquired powers, must assume great force. But the equality that is assumed and promised in the constitution of a democratic state does not exist in the individuals composing it. The most such a community can do is to try and afford equal opportunities to its unequally equipped members. The problem of poverty assumes a greater importance in a democracy than in an absolute government, inasmuch as in the former, conditions of life are less regulated by law and more by individual foresight and ability. Moreover, from this

Excerpted from Henry Dwight Chapin, "Preventable Causes of Poverty," in *The Forum,* 7 (June, 1889), 415–423.

it is evident that democracy does not necessarily help poverty; it simply places its conditions to a certain extent on a different basis. Classification of some kind there must be in society; that is the best which is based on the essential elements of fitness and unfitness. The natural mobility of such a society is at once a source of strength and of danger. Its strength is that it places no artificial bounds upon advance; its weakness that pure selfishness and ambition have no check. From the latter it follows that the accumulation of wealth, and consequent power, may remain in the hands of the minority; and the freest government may present relatively almost as much poverty as the most absolute. Poverty tends to be especially dangerous to social order under democratic institutions. With every freedom come greater wants and a greater sensitiveness to disadvantages.

The presence and growth of extreme poverty and a sharp struggle for subsistence, particularly in our large cities, force themselves upon the attention of physicians who serve in the hospitals and dispensaries erected for the poor. After seven years' service among the poorest classes of New York at the Bellevue and Demilt Dispensaries, it has seemed to me that physiology can afford the best preliminary solution of some of the problems of sociology. It is interesting to observe the opposite angles at which the poor and the rich look at methods calculated in any way to relieve distress. In spite of the cruelly close competition so often seen, and of the complaints made about the heartless methods of trade, many of the more prosperous classes of society have a sincere wish to relieve and elevate the very poor. Exactly how to do so most efficiently appears to be an open question. Numbers of the poor, led by theoretical thinkers, in looking for relief demand changes in fundamental economic laws that would require a disruption of society to consummate, and even a change in human nature itself. The rich who give freely of their money in charity find opportunity for doing good in founding benevolent institutions, endowing hospitals, establishing soup kitchens, etc. The line of all these laudable endeavors is more toward palliating the effect than removing the cause. In spite of the large sums annually donated for such purposes and the good thereby accomplished, the real problem of grinding poverty does not seem to have been touched. As the result of a little more than five years' work, the Charity Organization Society of New York reports 101,916 families who have sought or received relief, which is equivalent to 407,664 persons living in actual or simulated dependence. An investigation of this vast army of unfortunates will in very many cases show a combination of ignorance, inefficiency, and shiftlessness which are largely the results of physical and mental ill health.

What is to be the line of improvement in these cases? Is it to take the form of altered laws or attempts at a radical change of social order? Denison, an English observer and worker, incisively remarks that no ballot, nor manhood suffrage, nor confiscation of property, will ever make an ignorant man the equal of an educated man. No political dodge can reverse the decrees of nature; no municipal law can abrogate the supremacy of mind, nor deliver brute matter from its eternal subjection to it. Our efforts to relieve the very poor or degraded must take the form of personal effort aimed at individuals. They cannot be raised in mass by altering laws any more than by preaching or talking at them. We waste much time in this country boasting of equal rights. Is it not time we began to talk more about equal powers, or the way to try and attain them? The inequalities of society are largely the result of natural forces, which is another way of saying that there will always be many grades of prosperity and adversity. It will be a great help, however, to appreciate the line in which this difficult problem can be most rationally approached. It has seemed to me that public attention must be directed more and more towards the means of increasing and preserving physical, mental, and moral health, and vigor among the poor and unfortunate.

Much disability comes to many of the very poor from their utter ignorance of the simplest hygienic laws. This is perhaps most notably seen in regard to food. Granting the lack of means to purchase a variety of food, that form of nourishment should be selected which will yield the most energy and which can be easily digested. This is precisely what is not done. The most glaring instance of this is seen in the diet of the very young, at a time when growth is extremely active. The first few years of life are, physiologically considered, probably the most important period of our lives. At this time the young organism has impressed upon it the elements of future vigor or of early decay. Mistakes in diet are sure to result in seriously crippling growth and in lowering vitality. Such errors cannot be excused on the ground of extreme poverty, as the cost of proper nutriment—milk in some form—is less than that of the food so often substituted. The disease most commonly produced by this practice is known as rickets, which is accompanied by softening of the bones and various developmental changes that may very seriously handicap future healthy growth. An irritable and ill-balanced nervous system is a pretty constant accomplishment of this disease. At my children's clinic, out of one hundred consecutive cases lately presented for treatment, forty-three showed marked evidences of this taint, in addition to the illness for which medical aid was sought. This unfortunate condition is brought about not so much by unavoidable overcrowding and hardships, as by ignorance of the simplest elements of dietetics. The same disease is produced in the well-housed children of the rich by the same errors of diet. Various other unfortunate conditions may not be so easily obviated. A large proportion of the children of the poor in the great centers of population have scrofulous or tubercular ailments, due largely to foul air, overcrowding, and dirty surroundings. Yet care and cleanliness would do much to obviate even these conditions.

The first essential act in the effort to aid the struggle for subsistence among the poor, must be to try and dissipate some of the gross ignorance and shiftlessness that so often accompany it. The field of these efforts must be the individual family. All permanent relief must start and end in the family. This is the fundamental unit and basis of society and the state. No institution can take the place of the family. The domicile must hence assume great importance, not only as regards the efficiency, but also the morals of its occupants. Cleanliness, fresh air, good food, and the avoidance of too close a proximity of individuals, are alike necessities of physical and moral health. There are many difficulties connected with the subject of housing the poor. The problem is not so easy of solution as it looks. Reduced to a simple form, it would seem as if the destruction of bad tenements and the construction of good ones would settle the question. Unfortunately, the root of the problem goes deeper, for a change of domicile will not necessarily change the nature of the inhabitants. . . .

Any improvement in the domiciles must be accompanied by an improved development of the inmates. One conditions the other. The two must go hand in hand. Such improvement will be slow, as it involves undoing habits of life formed by years of cramped and foul environment. Undoubtedly it is easier to be clean in a clean place, but the essentially dirty will be dirty anywhere and everywhere. The similarity between the life conditions of the poor in the country and those of the same class in a crowded city has often attracted my attention. The same squalor, dirt, foul air, and crowding are seen, although with a very little trouble there could be in the country abundant expansion of the domicile and free entrance of pure air. A similar problem of ignorance and improvidence confronts us under the best as under the poorest of natural conditions. In some of the crowded districts of New York, however, there would undoubtedly be a beginning of improvement in the living habits of the people if they could have more room and better ventilation. The outer surroundings of life not only express but also impress the inner life. The inner degradation and the outer squalor react upon and confirm each other. The plan pursued by Octavia Hill in London appears to be in the right direction. A bad tenement is taken and gradually improved, somewhat according to the wishes, and always according to the needs of the inmates. Experience has shown that very radical improvements can gradually be wrought in defective tenement houses, and still a fair rate of interest be paid on the investment. In general, the right method of proceeding is to elevate people in their own sphere before trying to take them into a higher one that they cannot fill. After having procured better surroundings for the poor and inefficient, the next step is to educate and develop. This affords an apparently insurmountable obstacle. But is not that to a certain extent so because our methods have been wrong? Has there not been too much generalizing and not sufficient attention to detail? As already noted, the individual family must receive more attention. The mother must have impressed upon her the necessity of cleanliness, and must be instructed in the care of the house. She needs to learn about the selection and proper preparation of food that will yield the most nutrition with the least expense. The frying pan is the only utensil of cooking with which many a poor woman is familiar. The women must be instructed how to make the most out of scanty and unpromising materials. Many useful points can be taught them about clothing their children.

Plain sewing is an accomplishment unknown to many poor women, as any one can feelingly testify who has been repeatedly pricked by the pins used in holding their children's clothing together. In these and many other ways poor women could be made more saving in their homes, greatly to the betterment of the health and efficiency of their children. The line of effort is to try gradually to change many of their habits of life according to simple and well-known hygienic laws. The men exhibit fully as much want of thrift and thought in handling their wages as the women do in home affairs. No efforts are made to save even a little against a future necessity. Of foresight and self-denial they seem to know nothing. The 10,000 liquor saloons of New York get most of the surplus these people have over the actual necessities of life. There is this to be said, however, that bad air and poor food produce a craving for stimulation. Poverty is apt to produce drinking habits, just as drinking is pretty sure to lead to poverty. It is a vicious circle. The poorest districts have by far the largest number of saloons. If the houses of the poor were more cheerful and their food better prepared, doubtless the temptation to visit the saloon would be much lessened.

This brings us back again to the home as the source from which all lasting improvement must come. Whatever help is to be extended will here find a useful outlet. It will be impossible, however, to find out the real needs and weakness and possibilities of a family without visiting them. If intelligent help is to be extended, it must follow an investigation of the circumstances and character of those needing it. Owing to frequent neglect of this plan, the large sums annually devoted to charity have little real and lasting effect in aiding the struggle for subsistence. Something more than money must be taken to the poor and helpless. We must bring to them knowledge, foresight, a better judgment, a stronger will, and to a certain extent must exercise these qualities for them, until they begin to give evidence in some degree of possessing them. We must try to fortify them for a more effectual struggle, and not simply tide them over a week of hunger. It is well to relieve hunger, but a poor man will be just as hungry tomorrow and the next day as today. Sometimes about the only result attained by the relief of present distress is making sure its recurrence. This work of visiting and instructing the poor can, as a rule, be better done by women than by men. They have more tact and sympathy, and can accomplish results more easily, in an informal, friendly way. If a woman actuated by the right spirit is willing to visit a family regularly, much good can gradually be accomplished. Of course the results will be very slow. Her friendly instruction and advice can begin with the simplest rudiments of cleanliness, and slowly enlarge in many ways. She can try to inculcate habits of thrift, seek to procure work for the idle, endeavor to have the children brought up in a healthful manner and finally taught a useful trade; in short, make them efficient and self-supporting. As an aid to intelligence, the loan of books, papers, and pictures would do good service, and at the same time make the home more pleasant. Such means indirectly strengthen character by enlarging social opportunity. Any thing that will broaden the range of their social relations will be helpful to the poor. By treating them more as men and women and less as poor people, better results will be attained. Whatever is done, must be in the line of cultivating independence and breaking up the habit of dependence. If the furniture is rickety, they should be told to mend it as best they may, rather than have money given to purchase new articles. A three-legged stool had better have a fourth leg put in as a makeshift, than be superseded by a new stool that will soon be equally crippled. The doling out of help on all such occasions is a direct encouragement to improvidence and want of forethought. We must not by our help make the poor eventually more helpless. The only kind of help that does good and not harm is that which leads to self-help, and this efficiency and self-reliance must be the slow growth of a personal education. . . .

A knowledge of the needs, hardships, and temptations of those lower in the social scale will lead to sympathy and right help, and hence to the increase of feelings of human fellowship.

Is extreme poverty a continuous necessity? It is largely produced, on the one hand, by certain classes being physically, mentally, morally, and industrially unfit; on the other, by the selfishness of the rich, who, by inheritance or acquisition, are well supplied or equipped, and are not willing to help or strengthen the weak; who may even so control the sources of wealth as to increase the strain of poverty. It must be remembered, however, that the poor and the rich are equally selfish, but that the action of this trait in the latter class is far-reaching and disastrous. Out of these factors has grown up a strained and unequal social order, which, in itself, binds and perpetuates unfortunate conditions. The first line of improvement must be to educate, strengthen, and elevate, with the confident hope that the sociology of the future will witness a more equable division of wealth. No uncertain philosophy is needed in this work. Any one can engage in it, whatever his station or fortune, so long as others need help and strength.

Part VI

The State of the Union

The State of the Union

Assessing the "American character," and the state of the "American Experiment" were major pastimes for many distinguished analysts, both domestic and foreign. The United States seemed to be the future at work, with the material advantages and social problems that accompanied industrial growth, urbanization, and world interdependence. All observors agreed that the country's visible growth was striking. They also agreed that visible achievements hid many unexpected and baffling problems. But the American's traditional concern for perfectibility combined with willingness to embrace new ideas and techniques to fortify the era's optimistic outlook on life and the future. With a population of 75,000,000 in 1900, and of 105,000,000 in 1920, the country still seemed permanently spacious, her resources and will as limitless as the inherited promises of American life.

Chapter 20

The Americans in America

Herbert N. Casson

Is there an American race, with characteristics that are definitely its own; and what individuals, if any, may be said fairly to represent it?

These questions naturally suggest themselves in the final article of the series that has been running in this magazine for the past twelve months. They are important as well as interesting questions, and to get satisfactory answers I have collected the opinions of eminent foreigners, from De Tocqueville to George Bernard Shaw, and have interviewed all manner of people in various parts of the United States, from Joe, our office bootblack, to President Roosevelt.

After weeding out the views of extremists, who either over-praised our civilization or undervalued it, I have found a number of points upon which the majority were agreed. All, with three exceptions, believed that an American type of brain and character has already been developed—a type which could not have been

Reprinted from Herbert N. Casson, "The Americans in America," in *Munsey's Magazine,* 36 (January, 1907), 432–436.

evolved in any other country. They were also practically unanimous in saying that this American type was still unfinished in many respects, and that it was mainly the product of two factors —political liberty and the blending of many races.

In previous articles we have dealt with twelve main streams of immigration into the United States. We have spoken of the Canadians—I put the twelve races in alphabetical order—the Dutch, the English, the French, the Germans, the Irish, the Italians, the Jews, the Scandinavians, the Scots, the Spaniards, and the Welsh. But there have been other immigrants from every corner of the earth. In the public schools of New York, for example, there are children of eighty-one nationalities. It is the unique glory of America that it has taken all the rest of the world to make it. Ours is a cosmopolitan republic, the only one of its kind, either of ancient or modern times.

Americans Are Cosmopolitan

This may explain the fact, so puzzling to foreigners, that while Americans have as strong a spirit of national patriotism as any nation possesses, they are the most cosmopolitan people in the world. They are the least influenced by local prejudices, and the most firmly attached to their country as a whole. As Frederic Harrison observed, "the United States is one country much more than Great Britain is." No matter how distant his state, nor how strange his accent may be, an American is always a comrade in any group of his fellow countrymen.

It might even be said that the man of purest American blood is he who has the most cosmopolitan lineage. The late John Hay, for instance, who was often described as a typical American, was a composite, and was very proud of the fact.

President Roosevelt, too, tells with elation that he is a blend of half a dozen nationalities. In colonial days his Dutch ancestors intermarried with English, Scots, French, Irish, and Germans. His father was an Easterner, his mother a Southerner, and he himself was toughened and broadened into manhood in the West; so that he is both personally and officially a representative American.

This interbreeding of many nations has made us practically a new race. We are not Celts, nor Slavs, nor Saxons. Although we share the English language with the British peoples, we are not at all English in our mental makeup. We are building up a nation on a larger scale and on a higher plane than has ever been tried before; and this task has naturally given shape to our national traits and to our point of view. Such is the general opinion, so I have found, not only among Americans, but also among those foreigners who have studied us and our institutions.

"America is giving birth to a new race of beings," said an English writer as far back as 1837. "They are powerful and athletic, and more reckless of dangers than any people whom the world has seen. Love of liberty and love of adventure are their strongest passions; and they combine the intelligence of Europeans with the physical advantage of savages."

Generally speaking, the earlier visitors to America were most impressed by the spirit of equality and self-reliance. "Universal uniformity," said De Tocqueville, was the keynote seventy years ago. Every one had ambition, he observed. There was less genius and less ignorance than in Europe. Extreme refinement and extreme brutality were absent.

As might have been expected, Europeans were amazed to find that life and property were safe in a republic which had torn up by the roots the old ideas of caste and aristocracy. Here were millions of the sons and daughters of ordinary peasants managing their own affairs, and prospering better than the rank and file of any country had ever prospered before. In Europe, equality and liberty were new, even as theories; but here they were taken for granted, as much as the air and the sunshine. Every American was more or less of an incarnate Declaration of Independence. And yet, there was no anarchy, no lawlessness, no upsetting of social institutions.

In recent years, foreign visitors have said little about our liberty and equality, and most about the terrific pace at which we are moving. The latest French book on America bears the title "In the Land of the Strenuous Life," and its author, the Abbé Félix Klein, protests that he was almost stunned by the intense activity of Americans.

"In human energy the United States is the richest country in the world," says another Frenchman, Pierre Leroy-Beaulieu; and a third, Jean Frollo, of Paris, sums up a brilliant pen picture of America by asking: "Why refuse to admire this industrial activity which has outstripped all others, and which, if it does lack finish, is infintely more progressive and daring? America has its reverse side, like every other country, but I wish only to look upon the front, which is strong and resplendent with life."

Alertness Is a National Trait

One English author goes so far as to assert that an American's nerves respond more quickly to his brain than those of any other human being. An American, he says, feels strongly and feels everything. He is always on the *qui vive*—always ready for a full head of steam. Another British writer, William Archer, adds that "the great advantage which these superbly vital people possess over other nations is their material and moral plasticity. There is nothing rigid—nothing oppressive—nothing inaccessible to the influence of changing conditions." And Leschetizky, the famous Vienna pianist, who has taught students from many nations, says that "the Americans have the quickest perceptions."

Arthur Shadwell, of London, whose two volumes on "Industrial Efficiency" have lately been published, concludes that the usual method of advance in America is by brilliant leaps. He and several German writers agree in the opinion that we are too quick. There is too much speed for speed's sake, they say; too much slapdash and hurry-scurry. We chisel a railroad through enormous obstacles, says one of the Germans, and then bungle the train service through too much haste.

Ian Maclaren comments on American speed by saying that it deprives us of half the joys and satisfactions of living. It is too intense, too frantic. An American, he says, always regrets that he can do nothing with his feet while he is listening at the telephone.

Freedom From Monotony

Apparently, the European view is that we live in an atmosphere of constant agitation and excitement. We have no time to be either happy or unhappy. We abhor the humdrum and monotonous side of life, and our ideal of comfort is the sleeping car, in which we can hustle and sleep at the same time. Our favorite mottoes are: "Time is money"; "Boil it down"; "Do it now"; "Step lively"; and "No admission except on business." We chew gum and oscillate in rocking chairs to satisfy our nervous craving for "something doing." Risk and adventure are the spice of life to us, and instead of sitting down at the crossroads and saying, "Be sure you're right, then go ahead," we rush along at full speed and find out where we are going when we get there.

Next to energy, the second great American trait, so say our foreign critics, is self-reliance. "The American note," says a Scottish writer, Professor Muirhead, "is self-confidence." We are regarded as a nation of inveterate optimists. No defeat can destroy our faith in the future of America or in our own abilities. We have no patience with failure or despair. Even in our drama and our fiction we demand that every story shall have a happy ending.

Some writers say that our self-reliance is so extreme as to make us too much like an army of generals. "America is to the older countries," says one, "what vaudeville is to grand opera. Here there are stars, but no unity of action. It is all climax and no dignity, no background, no finale."

But it is conceded that in grappling with new situations the American displays the greatest readiness and presence of mind. He carries his habits lightly, cares least for red tape and discipline, and is better at initiative than at obedience. New surroundings do not abash him. He is seldom homesick, as the French and Swiss are. No one is a better traveler than he, and "any old place where he hangs his hat is home, sweet home, to him."

Coolness In Time of Danger

Several foreign editors have commented on the extraordinary coolness and buoyancy of Americans in time of sudden danger, such as was shown by San Franciscans last April. "The calmness of the Americans at the time of the earthquake was wonderful," said Pol Plançon, who was an eyewitness of the disaster. "They are the coolest people in the world in the face of danger; and the women are as calm as the men. I never saw such grit and nerve in any other country. Every one acted as if the whole thing were scheduled and he had been expecting it. No one lost his head for a moment."

With their magnificent city in ruins, the San Franciscans made a jest of their sufferings, and turned their calamity into wayside comedy. Even the telegrapher who first told of the earthquake sat in a tumbling building long enough to send a joke along the wires. "An earthquake hit us at five-fifteen, and our office is being wrecked," he said. "I'm going to quit, as the building is still shaking, and its me for the simple life."

One English author announces that "Americans have careworn but confident faces. They are a cheerful rather than a happy people." It is agreed on all hands that we have little reverence for the past. Our attitude toward antiquity is correctly indicated in Mark Twain's reverie at the tomb of Adam. As to the future, we look upon it as our best friend. Nothing is too big to daunt us; on the contrary, we are said to have "immensity on the brain."

No one intimates that we have in this country any of the snarling pessimism or revolutionism that is rife in many parts of Europe. The average American feels that when he disparages his country he insults himself. He knows that there are evils—plenty of them; but he shares in a sort of social self-reliance which gives him confidence that whatever is wrong will be put right.

"Don't grumble, boost," is quoted in Arthur Shadwell's book as one of our most typical maxims; and as a natural outgrowth of this confident and constructive spirit, says Shadwell, Americans have been the first to grasp the full significance of advertising and to lay themselves out to apply it. "In the art of advertising," he says, "Americans lead the world so successfully that no competitor is in the running."

American Idealism

One Italian has lately written a book on America entitled "The Land of the Almighty Dollar," but as a rule this old misconception is passing away. Several foreign authors have pointed out that rich Americans have broken all records in giving as well as in getting. Well-informed foreigners are now aware that business is supreme in the United States, not because Americans have more greed or lower ideals than other people, but because the dollar is our rough-and-ready way of representing achievement. What an American really values most is public opinion; and in spite of many apparent exceptions it is public opinion that awards the fortunes. The United States is practically a land without misers. Money is valued for what it will buy, not for its own sake; and as Americans have the highest standards of comfort and convenience, they require higher wages, higher salaries, higher dividends than other races.

"The true American is an idealist through and through," says Hugo Münsterberg in his "American Traits." He runs after money for the pleasure and excitement of the chase. In a nonmilitary republic such as this the path of ambition is a thoroughfare of commerce paved with dollars; and the man who might in Europe climb to be a peer or a prime minister becomes here the president of a railroad or the creator of a trust.

We seldom get credit for having much logic or philosophy. We have more schemes and fewer theories, it is said, than any other race. The commonplace American, who does things, is exalted above the genius, who is a theorist. But for driving a proposition ahead to success, whether it is logical or not, we are admitted to have no equals. We have become the supreme industrial nation by reason of our inventiveness, our willingness to risk large sums, and the intelligence of our wageworkers. No other country can show a building like our Patent Office, packed from basement to attic with nine hundred thousand inventions. Our plan of producing standardized articles in immense quantities has given us a telling advantage in the world market; and we have worked the miracle of reducing the labor cost while we were at the same time rasing wages and decreasing the hours of labor.

In education, this spirit of progressive common sense is shown in the study of subjects that are useful in public life. In literature, it appears in novels which have no mysticism or half-tints, and which are written in the most vivid and clear-cut prose. In archi-tecture, it has produced the twenty-story skyscraper. In agricul-ture, it is manifested in the harvester and the irrigation ditch. In religion, it shows itself in the institutional church and the Young Men's Christian Association.

As to whom we may call the typical Americans, I have found that public opinion has few clear ideas on the question. Every one is ready with a list of historic heroes, invariably including Washington, Lincoln, and Grant. President Roosevelt, naturally, is suggested as the best representative of the United States at the present time; and he, when questioned, quickly shifted the honor from himself to his Rough Riders, a body of men whom it would have been impossible to get together, he said, in any other country. A company of ten men of letters recently selected Emerson as the typical American author; and an English writer speaks of Edison as having the typical American face. But it would seem as if the word American were too large, too comprehensive, to be fairly represented in any single individual.

Emerson, as the author of the noble essay on "Self-Reliance," was the spokesman of his nation; but so also was Bret Harte, creator of "The Outcasts of Poker Flat." So were the serious Whittier and the witty Oliver Wendell Holmes, the polished Hawthorne and the slangy Artemus Ward. All that was best in New England was represented in the wit, common sense, and culture of James Russell Lowell; and the wide Middle West has spoken out in the quaint wisdom of Josh Billings, who was by turns a pilot, an auctioneer, a storekeeper, a school teacher, a cattledriver, and an editor.

Many Europeans mention Walt Whitman as the one writer who best outlines the American point of view. Whitman himself was insistent upon this point. "Every atom of my blood," he says, "was formed from this soil and this air; born of parents here, from parents the same, and their parents the same." Of living writers, Mark Twain, our humorous philosopher, is usually suggested as being the one whose genius is most essentially American.

Americanism a Matter of Quality

Judging from the individuals who are most often marked as typical of this country, Americanism appears not to be a matter of birth so much as of quality. On the one hand, we have a Levi P. Morton, whose ancestors arrived in the Mayflower days, and on the other, a J. J. Hill, who was almost old enough to be a voter before he set foot in the United States. The late Governor Pingree, of Michigan, whose ancestors had been in America for eight generations, was a man of the people, but not more so than the late Mayor Jones, of Toledo, who was rocked in a Welsh cradle, or Carl Schurz, who had become an American in sentiment years before he became one geographically.

In general, the typical American is said to be the man who is self-made and who has learned worldly wisdom by hard knocks. He must be shrewd and forceful, fond of big enterprises, a good talker, and many-sided. There must have been more or less of romance and adventure in his life. He must have loved and hated, and taken risks. Above all, he must respect public opinion and keep in close touch with the rank and file of his fellow countrymen. Such is the composite being who stands before the world as the proprietor of the United States—at least, so say his neighbors.

As it is said to require fully ten generations to fix any new characteristic, we may regard ourselves as still "under the head of unfinished business." Even unfriendly critics admit that our faults are those of a building half erected—of a statue that is partly buried in the marble. Youth is their cause, for the most part, and time is their cure. A young, four-generation republic like ours may well have many crudities; and especially a republic that is planned on such large and liberal lines. Having accomplished so much in less than seven-score years, who shall say that the problems of the future shall overwhelm us? "America," says Max Goldberger, "is the Land of Unlimited Possibilities."

The supreme work of developing an American type is still in process. When it will be finished, no one knows. The struggle is still on, between the noble and the base, the independent and the servile. As Luther Burbank, the plant wizard of California, has finely said: "We in America form a nation with the blood of half the peoples of the world in our veins. We are more crossed than any other nation in the history of the world; and here we meet exactly the same results that are always seen in a much-crossed race of plants—the best as well as the worst qualities of each are brought out in their fullest intensity. All the necessary crossing has been done, and now comes the work of refining and eliminating, until we shall get an ultimate product which will be the finest human race that has ever been known."

Chapter 21

America Revisited:
The Sensations of an Exile

William Morton Fullerton

... The recent electoral period, which I was able to witness at my
ease from the first of October to the end of November, must have
brought to the surface, even for a less detached observer than
accidentally I was free to be, cumulative illustration, and in fact
definitive proof, of what I have just been saying as to the discon-
certing blend of idealism and of practical sense in the American
people.

I had been back to the United States but three times in twenty
years, and before leaving in 1888 I had lived simply the idealistic
life of religious and bookish New England. From a New England
village I had passed to Andover Hill, and thence to the Harvard
of a quarter of a century ago. Before Andover I knew the prehis-
toric simple life of the New England village, with its town meeting, its Moody and Sankey revivals, its spelling bees, its
sleigh-rides. I knew a certain swimming pool in the Quaboag, and

Excerpted from William Morton Fullerton, "America Revisited: The Sensations
of an Exile," in *Scribner's Magazine,* 49 (June, 1911), 658-664.

I had camped of a summer at Lake George; but I was more at home on the shores of the Lake of Galilee, and I could draw a better map of the Acropolis of Athens than of the shoreline from Chesapeake Bay to the mouth of the St. Lawrence. Washington seemed as remote to me as Paris or London. Then came, for the boys of my generation who went to school and college, seven years of the sheerest idealistic instruction, every influence which tended to uproot us, as young Americans, from the society in which we were born. Rare were the special items, in the programme of our school and college work, which were adapted to prepare us for success in American life. Save for the periodic commotion caused by a presidential election, nothing happened during my entire American existence, up to the moment of my accidental settlement in Europe, which could throw any light on the changes which were taking place in American life. The generation of my elders had just terminated a four years' civil war, and they believed that they had settled for all time the destinies of the American people. I grew up in the sublime faith that the United States had already proved its *raison d'être,* and that nothing ever again could occur to arrest the triumphal advance of American democracy. Our superiority among the nations was so candidly and universally taken for granted, that we saw no danger lurking in the changes—the vast economic revolution—which were proceeding before our eyes, but which, indeed, we hardly noticed, so subtly did they begin, and so absorbed were we boys—*elsewhere*—by our studies.

I returned to the United States in October 1910, and I found the changes that had occurred during my absence to be so prodigious in quantity, and so varied in kind, that I might have fancied myself to have been dropped from an aeroplane into a new world, if I had not instantly detected, amid the cacophonous unrest of American life, the surviving leaven of the old-time spirit, the one clear note which was familiar. The founders of American society were idealistic even unto mysticism, but they were practical and hardheaded even unto sharpness, "cuteness," and canniness. Dr. Henry van Dyke, in his excellent lectures on "The Spirit of America," affirms what my most recent observation confirms, that the blended strains of blood which made the American people in the beginning "are still the dominant factors in the American people of today." And the intellectual and spiritual heredity has been communicated to millions of immigrants from all parts of the world. Throughout the electoral period of October and November, 1910, the spectacle was one which resembled nothing which has ever taken place elsewhere on so vast a scale. For an American who had lived for twenty years in foreign countries, it was rich in revelation as to the existence, after all, of a national spirit, capable of ultimately completing the work of unification, which even the Civil War, supplemented by the vast material coordinating forces of our time—railways, electricity, the printing press—have not yet sufficed to achieve.

A genuine passion for reform; a desire—oh, sometimes a very exhorbitant and fanatical desire—to make social relations and civic ideals square with a crude notion of justice and fair play; a recognition of the fact that the old confidence in the inevitable success and the obvious superiority of the American democracy was stupid and childish, and must give way before a systematic endeavor to work out a social ideal on a rational basis; the rejection of the former insolent attitude of *laisser-aller,* of devil-we-care fatuousness, for the adoption of strenuous and methodical tactics aiming at the organization of a really democratic existence, in which the useful impetus of characteristic American individualism, or the sacrosanct principle of state rights, would be curbed only insofar as individualism and state autonomy injured the interests of the vast community at large—all these signs of practical reform which had moralized politics, and which were peculiar to no political party, but which were as much the keynote of the speeches of the Democratic candidate for governor of New Jersey as they were the war cry of the Nimrod of the Republican party, bespoke a transformation in American conditions, which I repeat, would have made me feel that I was an exile in a foreign land, if I had not recognized in the ubiquity of this resolution to put the American house in order only a newer and more potent phase of the earlier high-minded sense of obligation to subordinate life to a moral ideal. The period of what the Canadians of the west call "making good," is ended, and the American population is now developing a critical spirit as to the quality of the results of their civilization. It is taking to politics with a "strenuousness" that has an ethical fervor. The legitimacy or illegitimacy of the triumphs of a rampant individualism—the literally imperial achievements of the unmolested money-getters who have built the railways and

founded the corporations of the United States; the problems of
national economic conservation; the present position and the future of American women; the moral aspects of tariff bills or of
banking legislation: such subjects as these are the recurrent
themes in all of the great popular magazines and reviews which
are read by hundreds of thousands of American citizens and gib-
bering candidates for American citizenship. This last fact is in itself
extraordinarily impressive.

I shall not soon forget a talk I had one afternoon with an editor
of one of the most successful of the American reviews. We had
been lunching at one of the Fifth Avenue hotels, and we came out
late into Central Park, where we lingered until sunset discussing
problems of American life. In the calm of that beautiful garden,
surrounded by palaces, while the beacon lights of the great city
leaped forth successively from its southern towers, this typical
American editor spoke to me, in a spirit of what the world is now
free to call Tolstoic idealism, of the high purpose that animated
him and his fellows. He spoke of their sense of responsibility as the
purveyors of right ideas to the vast avid American democracy. He
was filled with an exultant pride at the thought that he was helping
to mould the American man and the American woman. Then his
voice fell, and he expressed to me his dismay. He was playing,
blindly, he admitted, but, according to his lights, and up to the
limit of its possibilities, a considerable rôle in the piece so superbly
staged by the *Zeit-Geist* on American soil, a play of which no man
knew the end, any more than the crowd of those who, in the
streets of Rome, welcomed Caesar back from the Cévennes, knew
the end of the civilization of which they were the heirs, and in
whose promise they believed.

The sense of a moral purpose expressed in my companion's talk
—although from my European outlook I had looked upon him and
his fellows mainly as American businessmen, who were exploiting
the public taste without other aim than money getting—was a fact
which classed itself immediately with the general impression left
by the whole spectacle of American life. It was one with the cases
of advertised philanthropy on the part of the plutocrats, one with
the titles of the books published by the presidents of the colleges,
one with the inspiration of the sermons in the churches, and one
with the texture of the various planks in the political platforms. I
gathered the impression that save for the cult of sport—and, after

all, why had I to exclude this Hellenic passion from the category of moral impulses?—no activity is any longer conceivable in America except in relation to the whole problem of the national interest and of national improvement. Heedless individualism inspired by the merely selfish instinct of getting rich, or of being a success without thought of one's neighbor, is no longer American. The theory of "equal rights" has been tried and has been found wanting. The tradition of that persistent Jeffersonian principle is being hopelessly demolished by the lessons which Americans of the last generation have drawn from their political and economic experience. Everything that I saw, everything that I read, everything that I learned in America led me to believe that American society is already becoming what Mr. Croly, in his remarkable book "The Promise of American Life," declares that it must become, short of utter failure. It is becoming a democracy of selected individuals, who are obliged constantly to justify their selection. It is no longer, as Matthew Arnold called it, the home of *das gemein*. Its members are becoming united in a sense of joint responsibility for the success of their political and social ideal.

A Bossuet, rhetorically falsifying history in conformity with an *a priori* principle of preestablished harmony, might be tempted grandiloquently to recall that the north and south axis of the planet is that of the three great commercial and ethnic highways of world civilization: the Nile valley, the valley of the Rhone, and Manhattan Island, and to find a "providential" fitness in the fact that a self-conscious people, with a common political and social ideal, should be developed round each of these highways. But he would roll out anathema at one of the most characteristic aspects of American life, the universal interest in sport, the passion for play. Autumn in America today is, indeed, a season in which men and women of all ages, and not merely the youth who are donning the *toga virilis* and their beautiful partners, fleet the time strenuously as in a golden world. I was one of the wonderful crowd who assembled, in four different amphitheatres, round the football field, from Andover Hill by way of New Haven and Cambridge to West Point, to witness our young barbarians all at play. It was an imperial spectacle, and I had the sensations of a patrician. In my time at Harvard the great American public recked little of the fate of a university team when pitted against its rival. In America today the entire community participates in the tense curiosity with which the college graduates hasten, with the American women, to the tournament fields to see the youth—who are more like gladiators than like knights—do battle; and the newspapers of the continent, in the small as in the great towns, devote as much space to the games as they do to home politics, and infinitely more, to our shame be it said, than they do to foreign affairs. On the night after the collision between Harvard and Yale at New Haven, whence I had returned to New York by one of the thirty-seven special trains which had splendidly covered the distance on regulation time—a fact, in itself, of characteristic significance for a man accustomed to the mismanagement of certain European railways by the state—I found a letter from a friend who, addressing me from a small New England industrial centre, said: "You are at this very hour on the Field at New Haven watching the Football Game. I put it in capital letters for it seems to carry everything else before it. I went to the gas company's office today, and I found that all the clerks were sporting the colors of the two colleges. The crimson seemed to predominate, but many were wearing the blue. The shops are flying their flags. An inauguration of a president could not excite one-tenth of the enthusiasm."

It is necessary to have been able to confirm the truth of this statement with one's own eyes, not to suppose it to be cheap exaggeration. That thirty thousand or forty thousand people, among those who are doing all the serious things in the society of their time, should scramble for the privilege of watching a football game, that the fifty thousand others who are excluded from the privilege, more or less by chance, should envy them their good fortune, and that hundreds of thousands of others should be waiting at nightfall at the ends of the telegraph wires and in front of the bulletins posted up by the newspapers, to learn the result of a battle lasting ninety minutes, this is a fact which Europe could not understand. It is a fact of a Pindaric quality, and one which throws a beautiful light on the growth of the hero-cult in the civilization of Greece. America has not yet a national poet like Pindar, capable of celebrating the glory of a Boston, or a Duluth, or a New York, or a Richmond, or a Chicago boy in verses to the glory of these several cities, but it already has the pretext and the incentive for a Pindar; and when such a writer is born he will say in English, as his predecessor said in Greek, "Best of physicians for a man's accomplished toil is festive joy."

At Lenox, where the rich families of New York have created vast domains around their country houses, exactly as the rich Roman and Gallo-Roman colonists of the Burgundian highlands, by natural capillary advance up the Rhone valley, built in a wilderness villas crammed with the art treasures of Greece or of the home country; on Long Island, on the Connecticut slopes, in the *hinterland* of the Boston suburbs, or at Morristown, in New Jersey, where, in an atmosphere of admirable history, and in a region of beautiful hills and poetic waters, still other favorites of American fortune have organized a life warm with a rich comfort which only England's aristocracy had anticipated, the impression left upon the visitor is of another kind. It is distinctly that which Signor Ferrero, the historian of Rome, has chronicled in his notes on American society, and which he was bound to chronicle. The immense extension of the class which possesses the money to buy leisure, and enough money to buy leisure to be wise—even if all of them be not yet wise enough to buy that kind of leisure—is a new fact which illustrates once more how useful the economic key may be in order to penetrate the problems set by history. And these citizens who can now afford to play, are being imitated by the entire people, all of whom are "making money," or who are somehow enjoying the mysterious privilege of economic credit.

A quarter of a century ago most Americans doubted whether they had a right to play. None thought it "moral" to play long. This feeling was part and parcel of the emotion with which they clung to the validity of the then universally disseminated eleventh commandment: *Thou shalt not like.* Of that commandment not a shred remains. The Americans have issured forth from the dank Puritanism of their old-time places of worship and of study. They have come out into the open. They have striven to treat their moral rheumatism by a bath of sunlight. They are marching to the step of an imperial movement, and they are rapidly substituting for the old precepts a moral philosophy as realistic, as "pragmatic," as that which was born in the Greek *palaestra,* and which a little effort of mysticism might easily enhance—and no doubt will— with all the virtues of the famous *kalokagathos.* At present America has only reached the stage of calisthenics. With their emancipation from the book the Americans are—alas—recklessly shattering the language, inventing new idioms, sharpening certain words or destroying others; but they are, meanwhile, evolving in the open a physical type of man and woman which has already considerably altered the appearance of the race. The sons and daughters of my former comrades at Andover and Harvard have an average height from two to three inches taller than that of their fathers and mothers, and the faces and stature of the young women, as I beheld them assembled in thousands at the games, are those of a new physiological type, for which eugenics may have much to do, but which, as Mr. Gibson has so admirably seen, is being determined by moral rather than by physical causes.

"I haven't really created a distinctive type," Mr. Gibson said recently; "the nation made the type. What Zangwill calls 'The Melting-Pot of Races' has resulted in a certain character; why should it not also have turned out a certain type of face? If I have done anything, it has been to put on paper some fair examples of that type with very great, with minute, care. I saw the girl of that type in the streets, at the theatres, I saw her in the churches, I saw her everywhere and doing everything. I saw her idling on Fifth Avenue, and at work behind the counters of the stores. From hundreds, thousands, tens of thousands, I formed my ideal. And there is really, I believe, a reason why the woman of America has reached a higher type of beauty, just as she has undoubtedly reached a higher mental plane, than any other woman in the world. In American pictures woman has been notable because the artist has approached and treated her with an innate respect—with gallantry, if you care to use the term; but with no more than she deserves. American men pay homage to their women, actual homage. That is true and to their credit, but, sadly enough, makes them distinctive. The idea of the old-time European artist, and of many new-time artists on the other side, is that women can be just two things—mere toys or mere machines. The Englishman and the American—more notably, of course, the American—see that they are the biggest and best part of life, and treat them with regard and wonder. It is this appreciation that has helped our art more than any other one thing has. The men who harness women up with dogs will not advance much in their art; the men who place them where they rightfully belong will progress."

Dr. van Dyke, in the book already cited, denies the truth of the contention that any general and fundamental change has taken place in the human type in America. But that very trait of Americans, the expressions of which he analyzes so suggestively, their spirit of self-reliance—the characteristic which Professor Münsterberg calls the "spirit of self-direction"—has, according to my own observation, given to the male and female American face a *look* which distinguishes it from the expression of the British, French, or German face, and which climatic or other external causes would not have sufficed to induce. The British, Dutch, or Irish animal, *homo,* transplanted to America, might, perhaps, have become what Quatrefages declared he was becoming, a species of man resembling the North American Indian, if it had not been for the play of moral and economic factors which have saved him from the degeneracy. A new male and female beauty is being developed in America, and as I gazed on the types of men and women whom I saw at the University games, I was being prepared to agree with the artist whom I have quoted.

It is just because these handsomer and healthier Americans of the present generation whom I saw at the games are the descendants of men and women who had a peculiar endowment of energy, and a special training that was productive of real will power; it is, in a word, just because they have been able to preserve their *"forms of thought,"* that they have been able to expand with such abounding elasticity, and such a steady, and often insolent, optimism, within the vast limits of their continent, and that, furthermore, now that those limits have been reached, they have been able to develop the sanely sceptical attitude as regards the quality of their achievements, and the unflinching resolve to justify their belief in themselves, which are bound to strike any observer as characteristic of American society today. The horizon of a religious mind is not confined within the meridians traced on the surface of the earth. For many generations the Americans were profoundly religious, and their perspectives reached outward into spaces the reality of which was as characteristic as their remoteness. The Americans of today are less religious, notwithstanding the evidence afforded by the statistics of church membership. But the habit that they have acquired of taking the idealistic, mystical, religious, far view of human actions, their utter failure to comprehend the narrow *terre-à-terre* point of view, remains with them as a "form" of thought, which has been singularly and happily adjusted to the purely geographical conditions of their national expansion. And that particular "form" of thought is still the ample frame within which the American consciousness works and has its being. *An energy and a will to organize American society as a national basis is now being manifested as a spirit hostile to some of the most sacred political and social traditions of the people of the independent states.* This is the impressive implication of the whole wondrous spectacle of modern America.